PRAISE FOR *BUTCH IS*

"This book is illuminating, emotional, thought-provoking, and respectful.... The author's not afraid to roll up hir sleeves and get in the muck of it all: the fear, the anger, the passion, the loss, the delight, the benefits, the grief, the discovery, the confusion, and the certainty. This is the book that had me crying, laughing, and reading aloud to friends and my lover."
—*Books to Watch Out For*

"Human beings, as a rule, are pack animals. We seek the comfort and safety found in the company of commonality, the relief at being recognized for who and what we are. For those of us who have strayed from or strain against the dominant two-party gender system, finding one's true people can be a whole lot more complicated. This book is tangible proof that I belong to a sacred brotherhood. A rogue nation, complete with its own customs, code of honor, proud history, and even the odd secret password. Bergman's butch identity is not an apologetic footnote found on the second to last page of an essay on womanhood, or a misogynist romp through the locker room of unexamined masculinity. Somehow, the hero of this story manages to tiptoe through the minefield of gender theory in steel-toed boots, dodging dogma and crushing clichés, pulling off pirouettes around political correctness and sidestepping all stereotypes. This book should be a standard part of every butch's survival kit, right beside a sharp pocketknife, a clean handkerchief, and Dad's old Zippo lighter."
—Ivan E. Coyote, author of *Missed Her* and *Bow Grip*

"*Butch is a Noun*, and also a brave, whipsmart, and passionately human tour through a portion of the gender/cultural map normally marked 'Here Be Dragons,' to which author S. Bear Bergman is a most insightful, funny, and gracious native guide."
—Hanne Blank, author of *Virgin: The Untouched History*

"I'm not sure I can even begin to describe how good *Butch is a Noun* is: it's funny, and charming, and substantial—much as I suspect its author is as well. I found myself wishing that there were 365 of Bear's stories so that I could read one every day as a kind of meditation ... The charm of *Butch is a Noun* is that it takes its subject both seriously and with humor, but a gallows kind of humor, one that helps you survive a difficult world. There is no mistaking the undercurrent of sadness and anger, but the humor and love overwhelm both, as they should in any book about being butch. I really can't recommend this book more highly: it made me laugh first, then cry some, think seriously about the world, and by the end I felt I'd been given a great big Bear hug."
—Helen Boyd, author of *My Husband Betty: Love, Sex, and Life with a Crossdresser*

"Bear's poetry of butchness lets us see into facets of gender that usually aren't so transparent. And made me fall in love with butches all over again."
—Carol Queen, author of *The Leather Daddy and the Femme*

BUTCH
is a NOUN

essays by S. Bear Bergman

For Methea —
Thanks for being a part of speech.
xoo
Bear

Arsenal Pulp Press

Vancouver

BUTCH IS A NOUN
Copyright © 2006, 2010 by S. Bear Bergman

First published 2006 by Suspect Thoughts Press. Second edition published 2010 by Arsenal Pulp Press

Second printing: 2013

Book design by Shyla Seller
Photograph on front cover by David Wyse based on a concept by Zev Lowe

ARSENAL PULP PRESS
#101–211 East Georgia St
Vancouver, BC V6A 1Z6
Canada
arsenalpulp.com

The publisher gratefully acknowledges the support of the Canada Council for the Arts and the British Columbia Arts Council for its publishing program, the Government of Canada through the Canada Book Fund, and the Government of British Columbia through the Book Publishing Tax Credit Program for its publishing activities.

Printed and bound in Canada on 100% PCW recycled paper

Library and Archives Canada Cataloguing in Publication:

Bergman, S. Bear, 1974-
      Butch is a noun / S. Bear Bergman.

Also available in electronic format.
ISBN 978-1-55152-369-9

      1. Bergman, S. Bear, 1974-. 2. Transsexualism.
3. Female-to-male transsexuals. 4. Gender identity. I. Title.

HQ77.9.B473 2010   306.76'8   C2010-902975-5

RECYCLED
Paper made from
recycled material
FSC
www.fsc.org   FSC® C103567

For my beloved ocean-eyed girl, who gave me the courage to write this all down, with love always from your George.

CONTENTS

Acknowledgments

This book took three years and also a lifetime to write, and I owe a great debt to the people who saw it, and me, through. I am grateful beyond measure to my family—especially my parents and brother, who have supported all manner of endeavors about which they were deeply ambivalent. Heartfelt thanks are also due to Toni Amato, John Austin, Hanne Blank, Kate Bornstein, Sally Brown, SJ Cohen, Ivan Coyote, Malcolm Gin, Sasha Goldberg, Rabbi Jon Haddon, Andy Inkster, Mike Jenkins, Pamela Kimmel, Robert Lawrence, Sarah Katherine Lewis, Will Liberi, Zev Lowe, Skian McGuire, Zoe Medeiros, KJ Nichols, Cole Ouellet, Tori Paulman, Bobby Peck, Carol Queen, Coren Rau, Scott Turner Schofield, Gunner Scott, Peggy Shaw, Gwen Smith, Cole Thaler, and the Weiss family, all of whom have kept me going, kept me writing, kept me inspired, and kept me safe enough to do the hard parts. As much as I want to detail each of your individual invaluable contributions over the course of the last fifteen years, it would take another entire book. So, thanks for loving me so generously, for putting up with my nonsense, for kicking my ass when necessary, and for helping me walk through my fear with grace. I am both grateful and blessed to have such friends and mentors.

Thanks also to Leslie Feinberg for writing *Stone Butch Blues* (without which this book would not be possible), Greg and Ian at Suspect Thoughts for taking a chance on me, the Millay Colony, the Fund for Women Artists, anyone who ever emailed me to ask for a copy of that thing I read the night before, and to everyone who ever agreed to give me money in exchange for getting up and telling my stories.

Finally, thank you to Nicole, who has helped me to create so much possibility in my life. I'm trying my best to honor it.

A NOTE TO THE READER

This book was three-and-a-half years in the making, beginning on a dark street in San Francisco and finishing on a sunny afternoon in my studio at Millay. While writing it, I imagined at every turn the outlaws and heroes and storytellers I have loved and been loved by in my life. This book is my love letter to them all.

Here on the cusp of publication, however, there are a few things I would like to mention. I didn't realize I wanted to mention them until I had two conversations—first with my beloved friend Skian, and then with my brother Jeffrey. During the course of those conversations I found myself giving context to three choices I made in the writing of this book. In due course, it seemed wise to also share them with you, the reader. In no order, they are:

1. *This is only my experience.* It is my book about butch identity; I dearly hope that it resonates for other butches, for transmasculine folks, for all manner of types of people—but it is my experience, nothing more and nothing less. I do not imagine even for a minute that I am speaking for everyone, or even for anyone else, though in my heart I hope that I am speaking to a lot of other people. So this book is firmly situated not just in my butchness, but also in my other locations on every possible axis: race, religion, class, education, gender, and body. I know that my experience of butch is profoundly affected by those things, and I don't want anyone else to imagine (even for a minute) that I think I have written down the One True Way. I have written down my way, as honestly and completely as I can, which is all I can do.

2. *It is organized with butches in mind.* As I got to the point of structuring this book, I realized that I had a choice to make. I could choose a way that would be most satisfying for those who felt comfortable with butches and butchness already, or in a way that would be most comprehensible to people who were taking up the topic for the first time. I made what I consider to be a political choice, and I arranged the book for my brothers, as a point of pride, as a way to honor us all. That said, I am also completely delighted if you are reading this as an assignment for school, as a gift from someone who believes it will help you to understand hir better, or because you're curious. For you, I offer the following roadmap: start with "Fire the Copyeditor," then read "Defending Identity," and then "Being a Butch with Young Men." Then start back at the beginning and go merrily onward from there.

3. *I left all the sex in.* I have a great deal of respect for the power of sex and sexuality. Not just the power it has when it exists, but also the power it has when it is erased. I think that all of us have been punished for or with our sexuality in one way or another, and butches tend to get an extra big helping of this—both the punishment and the silence. For that reason, I chose to write one very explicit essay, to allow others to retain their eroticism, and to include them in the book. It is my way of breaking the shaming silences about sex that I have seen damage so many marvelous people. That said, I also believe that everyone should make their own choices about sex and sexuality, so if you do not want to read about explicit sex (or if you are one of my relatives), you will want to skip the essay entitled "Getting Fucked." You may also want to tread carefully in the pieces called "Laying Down with a Butch," and "Cocks." Although I feel clear that neither is

principally about sex, they do stop by there on the way to where they're going.

That's everything. Glad to have you. Go read.

We want to pass things down. We want heirs, and if I cannot have heirs of blood then I want heirs of spirit; I want you, when you are grown, when I am gone, to have parts of me. This is the first thing, the handkerchief. In its way, it is emblematic of the butch heart—it is something you carry with you at all times for the express purpose of giving it away when it is needed.

I KNOW WHAT BUTCH IS

I know what butch is. I know, and I'm going to tell you, so listen up and take notes. First of all, butch is a noun. And an adjective. And a verb.

Butches only ever wear jeans and boots, except if they're wearing suits, and they keep their hair clipped down to a flattop you could putt off. Except if they have to for work. Or if they want to for sex. Or if they want to for some other reason. But otherwise it's denim and leather and butch wax, kid, and don't you forget it. Unless you're vegan.

Toughness, even at the expense of gentleness, is a butch trait. Butches are outlaws. Also gentlemen. Gentlemen who open doors and pick up checks and say "after you" and hold your umbrella over you in the rain while the water drips down their sleeves. But butches not gentlemen if being a gentleman means imposing on the unsuspecting their sexist modes of acting out the cultural paradigm of the helplessness of women. Except if the unsuspecting are crying and need a handkerchief, or elderly and need a seat to sit down in, then it's all right. Probably. But butches should never wait for a femme to tell them specifically that it is all right to behave in a gentlemanly fashion, they should just go ahead and do it because femmes like a butch with confidence, unless it turns out that she finds it offensive and feels as though you have imposed your gender fetish on her, you arrogant bastard.

And butches are monosyllabic, until you get to know them, which they will not allow but want, or will allow and want, or will allow but don't want, or won't allow and don't want, so you may or may not get to know them, but you should try, or not. But butches are monosyllabic because all that talking is girl stuff, you know? Butches grunt in answer to questions; they speak sharply and emphatically. They do not share, process, or explain because these are activities that bring nothing but trouble, unless they are bringing relief to the troubled heart of a butch carrying around too much hurt or pain, though butches do not actually feel pain; they're tough enough to either slough it off like dead skin or deal with all of that themselves. Unless someone wants for them to be emotionally available, in which case they can feel their feelings even though the presence of feelings is suspect in the first place, but they must stop immediately as soon as someone else is having a tough time so that all their resources can be directed to soothing that person.

I know what butch is. Butches are not beginner FTMs, except that sometimes they are, but it's not a continuum except when it is. Butch is not a trans identity unless the butch in questions says it is, in which case it is, unless the tranny in question says it isn't, in which case it's not. There is no such thing as butch flight, no matter what the femmes or elders say, unless saying that invalidates the opinions of femmes in a sexist fashion or the opinions of elders in an ageist fashion. Or if they're right. But they are not, because butch and transgender are the same thing with different names, except that butch is not a trans identity, unless it is; see above.

Butches are always tops. They always fuck the girls, and, for that matter, their partners are always girls; there is no such thing as a butch who is attracted to men. Well, transmen, but that's just butch-on-butch repackaged as faggotry. But no non-trans-men.

Unless the butch in question is a non-trans-man, then it's okay. Except that non-trans-men cannot be butches, because butch is a queering of gender that assigned-male people cannot embody, unless they occasionally can, in which case they have to be gay men. Or the partners of femmes. Or not. But no one with an assigned-female body can be a butch and do it with assigned-male men. Unless they're femmes. Or butches. I'm really putting my foot down on this one.

I know what butch is, and butches definitely, absolutely, do not get fucked, even if it feels so good to have someone slide in sweet and hard and rock them just right. They might eat pussy but they never suck cock, because licking pussy is chivalry without pants, and, of course, any butch would want to do anything to please the femme in hir life, if there is a femme. Which there has to be, in order to be a true butch, except if there does not have to be, but you cannot be a misogynist about it either, which a lack of interest in femmes and their attendant delights may be read as—if there is a lack, which there shouldn't be. But anyway, cocksucking is about ownership and dominance, so butches must always be the ones having their cocks sucked, unless the owner of the cock being sucked by a butch is tied to something, but if a butch were tying down someone with a cock of some variety then the above rule would quite likely be violated, and I think I've been very clear about that, so never mind.

Butch has a lot of privilege because butches pass as men a lot, and butches also have a lot of privilege in the queer community because butch reads as queer and femme doesn't always, and being able to pass to keep one's self safe isn't privilege if you're a femme but it is if you're a butch. Unless this is a butch who can pass as a heteronormative woman, in which case ze's not really a butch anyway because no butch could do such a thing. Except that some of them can and also having kids really helps, even though no butch could have kids because of the rule about not getting fucked and also because that's a femme's job, but not everyone really understood their butchness all the way along and also sometimes there are fertility issues and also sometimes there's not a femme so we'll grandfather in some children but we'll be suspicious of those butches. Unless they're really great butch dads of whatever sex, in which case we'll think it's the damn cutest thing in the world and punch them on the arm, or if they're awesome butch moms we'll make approving comments about their ability to raise feminist men, but otherwise no children and no heteronormativity for sure, except for assigned male butches who do not exist.

Besides all of that, the butch pays. If there's only one butch on the date. Unless the femme wants to. If there's a femme present. If there's a femme present, the butch pays unless hir paying would upset the femme or unless it creates class issues for the butch or patriarchy issues for the femme. Or if it's two butches on a date, which they shouldn't be. Or they should. In any case, they arm-wrestle for it. Except in such situations in which a public display of aggression on the part of butches, or an interaction which may be read as such, could potentially be detrimental to the community, to the mental health of those witnessing the act, to the butches themselves for feeling compelled to act out normative masculine-gendered conflict-resolution tactics, or to the glassware of the dining establishment, which so often gets broken. But otherwise, the butch always pays, and there's just no getting around that.

I know what butch is. Butches are a brotherhood, or possibly a sisterhood, which would be a marvelous way to reclaim butch's roots in the lesbian community except some butches were never part of the lesbian community and some were but aren't any more, but placing masculine identities on butches is disrespectful, except when it's desirable, but anyway, butches are a tribe, a tribe of people who have been maligned endlessly for, and in fact forged an identity in part out of, not fitting the gendered expectations of the culture in which they exist (until or unless they work to pass as men, which always or never or sometimes happens and is absolutely a great or problematic thing), so butches are very open to gendered variations in others and would never, ever try to make another butch feel like shit for having displayed a behavior which does not fit the microculture's standard of what it means to be a butch, which is a useful or idealized or ridiculous or just plain complicated standard, so it should be adhered to, or critiqued, or aspired to, or not. Butches would also certainly never try to school younger butches in ways that are angry and dangerous because they feel like the process of toughening has disappeared from modern culture and butches need to be tough, dammit. Butches who do those sorts of things either are Real Butches or are Not Real Butches, depending who you ask.

There, that should be perfectly clear.

FIRE THE COPYEDITOR, OR POSSIBLY THE AUTHOR: A FEW NOTES ON PRONOUNS

Though English has evolved away from gendered nouns in most cases (boats being one of our last vestigial exceptions), we are nonetheless deeply attached to gender when it comes to people. We have a masculine set of pronouns for men (*he, him, his*) and a feminine set for women (*she, her, hers*). It, popularly discussed in grammar texts as a neutral pronoun, is not used for people or is used only to express one's great distaste for the person in question, often a person of indeterminate, complicated, or confusing gender. He's a boy, she's a girl, it's a table, and there we go.

The way that English sentences are constructed, when we're talking about a person, pronouns are used quite a bit. It is very difficult, as any closeted person who has ever tried to explain what ze did over a weekend will certainly tell you, to say even a few sentences about another person without using gendered pronouns. You end up constantly using the person's proper name and sounding like you are being translated from English to some other language and back again:

Well, Pat and I went to get Pat a new car, which Pat has been needing for a while because Pat's old one is more than ten years old, and Pat ended up getting a 2002 Camry. Pat really likes it.

Or everything has to be constructed in the passive voice with odd, pronoun-avoiding jumps passed off as colloquialisms, and you end up sounding like you're being heard through a poorly maintained fast-food drive-through speaker:

Well ... went to get a car because the old car has needed replacing for quite a while. More than ten years old, you know. A 2002 Camry got picked out, and it seems like it'll be a good choice.

Neither one's really a great moment in language. Some people opt for the plural-pronoun-as-neutral-singular option:

Well, I went with my friend ... so they could get a new car. They'd had this old one for more than ten years, so they really needed something newer. They got a 2002 Camry, and they seem really happy with it.

But that always sounds to me as though either you are dating someone with multiple personalities or you're polyamorous, either of which is a dandy thing as far as I'm concerned, but not what we're aiming at here. Why am I bothering to tell you all of this? Because before I introduce you to your new friends, the gender-neutral pronouns, I want you to understand why they are useful and necessary things. I want you to feel in your mouth the hesitation, the frustration, the stumbling over gendered pronouns that you must do when speaking about a person whose gender[1] is neither man, in which case masculine pronouns would be likely appropriate, nor woman, in which case feminine ones would probably be.

My theory is that butch is a noun, a gender all its own, something which cannot always be described within the confines of the bigendered pronoun system we have now. In an attempt to honor butches of whatever sex, whatever pronoun they may personally prefer (and my experience of butches is that they may prefer either, both, these gender-neutral ones, or, in some inventive cases, may have made up their own), I have chosen to use gender-neutral pronouns when referring to butches-in-general in this book. It feels much like butches do to me, in that so many ways

---

1. For a cogent and entertaining explanation of the difference between sex and gender, please refer to *My Gender Workbook*, by Kate Bornstein, pages 35–39.

of gender all combine and collide and get expressed, all of which get divorced from their traditional genders to come and shack up with Butch. It seems congruent to use language that has the most possibility inherent in it. Those gender-neutral pronouns are (drumroll, please): *ze* and *hir*. Let's meet them; you'll be spending a lot of time together during the balance of this book.

Ze, pronounced *zee*, like the twenty-sixth letter of the alphabet if you speak American English, is used as the subjective pronoun—that is, instead of she or he. "Ze went to the store," "What kind of shoes is ze wearing?" "Does ze have relatives in Bulgaria?" and so on. Also, ze is an incredibly useful solution to the problem, when writing formally, of having to write s/he or he/she when talking about a person of unknown gender, now that the "universal masculine" has, we hope, gone the way of the dodo but with much less lamentation.

Hir, pronounced *here*, is the objective and also the possessive pronoun, and is used in place of the feminine pronoun *her* or *hers*, or the masculine pronouns *him* or *his*. "Ask hir for the time, please," "It's hir truck, not mine," "Have you thought about asking hir on a date?" In formal writing, *hir* solves the his/her, her/him problem very neatly: "Before an applicant can be considered, hir entire portfolio must have been received and processed," "If you encounter a local resident, you might consider asking hir to help you find one of the sweet springs; they are a wonderful treat."

By using gender-neutral pronouns in this book (except in cases where I know the butch in question personally and know hir specific preferences with regard to pronouns at the time of writing), I am trying to open up a space in the language for people who are not man- or woman-gendered, in much the same way as I am trying—by writing this book—to open up a space for a gender that is not man or woman in the way people think. I have been warned that people will find it jarring. I am told by people who almost certainly know more about such things than I do that innovations in language come very slowly, that stubbornly choosing to use such a new form will make this book inaccessible.

It is true that I am stubborn. It is a butch trait. We have to be stubborn in order to exist in the face of cultural norms, or there would be no such thing as butch. Butch, a moment of lovely deviation from normative gender. Butch, standing apart from what is expected or accepted and waiting to see if you're interested enough to come too. It is my butch sensibility that enables me to feel roughly the same way about offering you, the reader, gender-neutral pronouns as I do about offering anyone an invitation to my sexuality: an attitude that can best be described as a "come hither or fuck off." I have already invested my trust in you by writing this book, and, by opening it, you have already decided to give me a shot. Now we take the next deviant step together, and I try to describe and explain what it means to me to be a butch (n.).

We do not have nearly enough language to make this easy. Striking out into the beginning of a discussion of butch as a gender, as a way of being in the world, I am acutely aware of all the words I need that I do not have: a dozen kinds of longing, thirty shades of pride, a hundred kinds of honorable intention. I bring my skills, such as they are, to bear as best I can, but I am still fumbling. I do have gender-neutral pronouns, and you're willing to read them and understand what they mean, so here we go. Here we go.

DEFENDING IDENTITY

I write and speak and go on and on at great length about my identity on a professional basis with my performance and writing work, literally touring the country for money telling interested queers and college students what my identity is, how I think and feel about identity in general, and how the two do or do not go together. My identity, my complicated butch identity, this crazy identity that requires an hour, two charts, and a graph to explain, is the commodity I use to make my living. I am an identity whore.

This is all very well and good during my workday, when solicitous professors ask politely by which pronoun I might like to be introduced and/or addressed, and students take notes on what I say and do and talk about it in class the next day, but that accounts for a very small percentage of my public life. The rest of the time, at the supermarket and the airport, on the street and anywhere else I go, I am not in control of my identity. I am being identified by others and living with the results.

I'm lucky, and also skilled. I have good theater training and a good understanding of gender. If I really care to, I can get people to see me as whatever gender I want. But that's if I'm willing to perform a recognizable identity, a recognizable gender. Young Professional Woman. Dutiful Granddaughter. Nice Young Man. Whatever. These are genders that the heteronormative world recognizes, and when I dress for them and pitch my voice appropriately for them, and hold my head and my hands just right and stand and sit and walk with care and attention to them, I can get recognition as something known.

This is sort of like going to a donut shop. There are the do-nuts. The top ten kinds are familiar, then another ten are variations on a theme; you know chocolate frosted, so if you see maple frosted or even motor-oil frosted, you know what you're getting, where the point of variation is. You pick what you want, based on your degree of adventurousness in donut eating and what you've had before, and that's it. This is what I do when I am invested in having my gender read a certain way. I plan, I prepare, I smear myself in chocolate frosting, stick on a sign that says "chocolate frosted," and do what I need to do.

But in the day-to-day, I am not preparing. I am just quietly living my life, picking up my dry cleaning or going to the lumberyard or taking a walk or what have you, and in that process people see me, and when they do, they are looking at me, matching me with their top ten familiar flavors and making an identification based on what point of variation they do or don't see. They do this entirely on their own and without consulting me at all, except for the exciting instances in which someone demands: "What the fuck are you?"

And so I am constantly scanning people to see how they are identifying me, how close it is to my actual identity, and making decisions on the fly about how to deal with that information. I read and respond in the same instant, a response determined by where I am, who I'm with, and what I'm doing.

Sometimes the cussed outlaw in me chafes at being identified too quickly and wants to queer the waters by performing gender in ways that do not go with the identification I'm getting. But my practical brain intervenes in the Fool's errand; there are times when it does not seem especially safe and comfy to pop up and defy people's expectations. In those moments, my ears twitching and skin alert to changes in the weather, I look for how I'm being seen and live up to it, step right into it and perform it until I am, say, no longer in the store of a roadside gas station in way-upstate someplace that has a gang of white-hatted teenaged boys loitering out front of it. That's not when I want to have a teaching moment around gender. That's when I want to thank fucking G-d for the voice lessons that taught me how to pitch my voice down into a respectable tenor and then get the hell back into my car. It's when everything slows down a little bit, and I scan each face for a millisecond to see whether the eyes under the cap brims are interested or inert, whether I have blipped their radar at all; when my heart beats faster and my vision narrows and I feel like I should sniff the air, that it might give me a clue. This is sometimes. This is when being identified gets dangerous. When my identity becomes dangerous.

But sometimes being identified becomes play. Or theater. Sometimes it's that, too. Sometimes I see how people are identifying me and I like it, or it tickles me in that moment. I inhabit it and play it up big, bringing out all the parts for it and walking around in it, like at the department store when I go in to pick up something for my wife and the nice ladies at the makeup counter treat me like a big dumb guy, and so I bumble around and act befuddled and bewildered and oh-so-grateful for their kind assistance. Even though the truth is that, after a decade of femmes in my life, I know the difference between an astringent and an exfoliant, thank you, and even if it weren't for them I grew up as a Nice Jewish Girl. Makeup counters and I have never been strangers. But still, I shrug and smile while they marvel over the modern man who is willing to be caught at the Estée Lauder installation at all, and they pat the back of my hand and send me away with big smiles, 'cause they think I'm so damn cute.

Or when I'm needing to get things done right and right away, and I'm in maximum efficiency mode and the fellow to whom I am addressing my problem sees a modern professional girl and my voice modulates into a smooth musical pitch and my hands rest lightly on the counter and I am being firm but kind with him about whatever the issue is, listening sympathetically to his explanations of how hard it will be to solve the problem and leading him in five deft steps to the solution with tiny gestures and frequent employment of phrases like, "Is this making sense?" until he thinks the whole thing is his brilliant idea and I am just so glad we got it worked out, and he wants to pat me, but doesn't, 'cause I'm a girl and that might be inappropriate behavior.

Either way, though, any which way, I am being identified by someone else, unless I keep the sartorial equivalent of five kinds of frosting and the matching labels with me everywhere I go. Which makes me wonder: why exactly I am spending so much time and energy talking about my identity, when as soon as I step away from the lectern I lose so much of my control over it?

Embracing the Zen of identity seems less tiring, for sure, less taxing, and certainly more logical, and yet the more I get identified in the world, the more it makes me want to have that moment of determination all for myself; the more it makes me want to offer the people I encounter a much wider understanding of potential identities so that when I am seen on the street I am understood by more and more people as what I am: a butch.

The more I feel how little agency I have in the moment of

identification, the more I want to encourage others to speak about our identities, making them understood, baking our identities at home rather than buying them prefab at the store, and putting whatever we want into them. It means frosting them carefully and beautifully and labeling them with our own queer names, and taking big delicious bites and smacking our lips and rubbing our full queer bellies conspicuously in front of people still nibbling away on store-bought. Giving them tastes. Telling them how it's done and showing our crazy, private recipe books and letting the secret ingredient out and being patient when the first tastes are so foreign to their homogenized palates. Letting them come back again and again for another taste, all the while feeding each other the richest, best, sweetest bites and laughing because it's so, so good.

TRANNY BLADDER

I have tranny bladder. You know what I mean, right? The amazing ability to go approximately forever without needing to pee? I am the person who leaves the house, has two meals with a soda and a glass of water at each, returns home eight hours later and finally-pees, after having stood around several times, at least after each meal, trying not to look like a sexual deviant (you know, in the bad way) while hanging around the restrooms waiting for my date to finish up. I wait to pee until I can get to a "safe" bathroom, safe bathrooms being the kind in which I am not screamed at to get out immediately, where I am not followed in by the lurking-outside-waiting-for-his-daughter father looking to kill me slowly, and that I can use without an NYPD officer and an Army private on Homeland Security detail (just, you know, for example) being called in to look at my ID.

This mostly means waiting until I am no longer in a public place, and so I just wait. The years and years of waiting, and holding it, have taken their eventual toll, it seems. And so, like so many butches I have known, like so many of my trans-siblings, I have developed this miraculous ability to just … wait. I mean, we are also probably all dehydrated. You do not see deviantly gendered people walking around with Nalgene bottles, getting our sixty-four recommended ounces as we go through our days. I am sure that somewhere there is an argument to be made that the trans community as a whole is a little cranky because we could all use a nice big glass of water.

It makes both my grandmothers crazy to the point of neurosis, by the way. They think there is something the matter with me (you know, in the bad way). They look at me with eyes full of the measuring medical expertise that apparently comes with being a Jewish grandmother, and they shake their heads and quiz me like a six-year-old with an unfortunate habit of wetting myself.

Did you go? Do you need to? Are you sure? Did you try?

What do I say? No, Nana, I don't need to use the bathroom, and I will not for the entire foreseeable future because I'm sure as hell not using a women's bathroom here in South Florida, which is populated entirely by slender blonde girls and elderly women with failing eyesight? This is leaving aside entirely, for the moment, how angry it makes me to write about these things—drinking water, and pissing it out—as though they were not the *most* basic kinds of freedom, as though even political prisoners both here and abroad didn't have more and better freedom to drink water and piss it out than most of the transfolk I know do, or did at some stage. This is not engaging what it feels like to be quietly peeing in a women's bathroom and hear, after a knock at the stall door, "Sir?" or pounding and then, "What the fuck?"

No matter how I pitch my voice when I answer, even when I use the most head-resonant and high-pitched voice I have available to me that doesn't make me sound like Flip Wilson on helium, I still have to open the door and show someone my ID and smile my beta-wolf smile at them, while the alpha inside me is tearing a hole in my chest trying to get out and teach them a lesson about manners and respect.

When I get harassed in the Ladies' room, or the cops are called, I can produce an ID with the telltale F and add the story to my collection. Transgressing in the Gents can have its consequences, legal or chillingly illegal. Men's rooms can be more forgiving because the culture of a men's bathroom insists that men not look at the others in the restroom lest they be labeled fags. Most curious looks can be deflected with a quizzical but hostile glance that seems to convey the idea that a man looking at you as you enter might have some sort of queer gaze.

Transfolk wait for the day that they can use the restroom with members of their chosen gender without problem or comment, and swap pissing stories and methods like trading cards in the meantime. I have heard arguments made that bathroom experiences are the defining measure of trans-ness: have you ever had anxiety, apprehension, or problems using the restroom which corresponds to your assigned-sex-at-birth? Then you're transgendered in some fashion. It's not the worst idea I've heard.

The bathroom is where gender performance meets public perception with a resounding *thwack*, one that sometimes hurts and sometimes reverberates down my butch life in unexpected ways. It's where I have to make a public declaration and I can never be sure which one might match what people are expecting from me, and the consequences for being wrong are always so unpleasant, because the wrongness is so basic. I am wrong in the world, they're saying, wrong to have fooled them, to be a coyote among dogs and cats, to stand in gender's doorways and whistle, and they'll make me pay while my pants are down, if they can. When I use a bathroom in public, I piss with one hand on my belt buckle so I can make it into a weapon if I have to.

Tranny bladder is my saving grace.

TAXONOMY

We need to know about gender so we can know about language. Otherwise, why does anyone care how I identify? You see me, yes? You take in my gendered cues, my physical presence, my space and persona, and unless you want to talk about me, or maybe fuck me, you know all you need to know. Whether or not you can understand me in this way, you can still see me. To borrow: *I* has no gender, neither does *you*. Only the third-person pronouns, the oh-lookit pronouns or the ooh-baby pronouns, depend on gender, depend on being able to read and understand someone's cues and come up with an answer. Only the third person requires a final reading on a gauge, a matrix measurement that reveals something to put your hands around (like my throat) or your mouth around (like my cock) when talking about me.

Without a gender, without language, people revert to a vocabulary of gestures, pantomiming me between their hands, the breadth of my shoulders, the swell of my breasts, my ears with earrings in them, the length of my stride. Without a gender upon which I can be fixed with steel pins, like a winged insect to a board, I flap around the room, maybe entrancing, maybe beautiful, but maybe dangerous, maybe terrifying. The pins of language are so short, and my wings so invisible with the quickness of their beating, that I evade them until I choose to land, choose to explain myself, or until I get beat out of the air. I try to alight before I can be caught, try to show myself, but it doesn't mean that someone doesn't have a little jar waiting to stuff me into with nothing for company but a leaf and a branch, even though I eat from flowers, or sweaters, or things that cannot be seen by the human eye; take my comfort behind the bark of a tree, or the ear of a sleeping wolf. Maybe there's a reason that the study of insects and the study of words are only one letter apart, and I can never remember which is which.

I don't want to be killed in order to be classified, don't want to end up like Tyra Hunter, or Brandon Teena, wrestled down out of the sky and pinned down by flesh or steel in order to be identified and shoved into the last box I'll ever occupy. I've fought my whole life to stay out of them, and I'll for sure fight like hell to stay out of this one, too, even though I know that this culture, this time, has a love affair with boxes and they're fitting me for one, one way or the other, sooner or later.

So I try to get big. I try to embody or encompass so many things, so many genders, so many ways of being, so many abilities and sensibilities, methods and modes that I won't fit inside any box they have, and while someone's out back with the hand tools trying to build a bigger one I grow larger still, fat on the words I eat and the people I taste and the places I migrate and spawn, evolving all the time, trying to stay ahead of the charts and workbooks, getting strong on the paradigms I break and the hearts I lift and the boundaries I push through until I'm a little bit too much for the box someone's just finished and they have to try again tomorrow. Meanwhile I become a larger and larger target, it seems, a bigger spot against the white expanse on which I sit, but at least when I'm taken down they'll have to preserve and study me, a marvel in a jar, a glass jar, a little bit of learning in the form of wonder.

I'd rather donate my body to science. Jars let the light in.

WALKING WITH GIRLS

When I walk by myself, I notice that the mutual avoidance pact of public passage on sidewalks and streets is in effect. I walk, keeping my eyes up, like nearly everyone does, and I adjust myself minutely as I go to make sure I don't crash into other pedestrians. They're all doing the same. From time to time someone very invested in being seen as a badass purposefully performs the act of not adjusting for anyone else, making others adjust for him or her. (There is a whole book to be written about the ways in which gender affects people's understanding of their responsibility to yield space in the world: sitting on subways, waiting in lines, walking on the street and anywhere else public performance of gender occurs.) But mostly we stay out of each other's way, me and the rest of the walking world.

When I walk alone, very little problem.

When I am walking with a pretty girl, however, or sometimes a femme boy, things change; my gender changes. If I am seen as a butch, or as a man: that is, as someone who is understood to have women as the object of my desire. If I am seen as a butch, or a man, I am now—to some minds—walking with someone who is under my protection and who is in my possession. Whatever critiques of gender and culture apply to that assumption, and they are numerous as the grains of sand, they do not always assert themselves in the walkaday world. The girl, as they say, is mine, and my gender performance has to change in order to meet that expectation.

This is partly my own ego, of course. I want to be visible as tough enough to possess and defend a femme who is entrancing enough to become the object of someone else's desire, but it is equally a measure of protection for the femme in question. What if the same person sees her walking alone tomorrow? The reality of violence against women is huge and close; I have been a target of it and I have lived close to the aftermath. I have interposed myself as gracefully as possible in any number of such situations, and I have been used as a safe harbor by friends and strangers alike to deflect unwanted attention. I have seen all manner of men and boys melt away when I appear and rest my hand lightly but familiarly on a waist or neck, looking friendly and interested and present and big in my body. It rises up in me unbidden, every time, the knowledge that keeping this femme safe when I am not present may have something to do with the public perception of who might be in the wings to protect her.

It's a fine line. I don't want to be overtly challenging, don't want to create in someone else an animal need to, for lack of a better metaphor, piss on my territory; I just want to mark it and stand there and look tough enough to defend it, if necessary. I just want to create a less inviting environment, based on the crime theory that a miscreant will look for the easiest way of getting what he wants. An elderly woman is mugged before a middle-aged woman, a house with a shoddy lock gets burgled before one with two locks and a big dog in the yard.

I don't want to be a challenge, either; don't want to be an alarm system and floodlights and a gate that makes someone want to test his skill and wit against it. I just want to be a big dog in the yard. Next time you come 'round, the dog might be inside. Might be at the vet, might be mama's li'l puddin' pup and no threat to anyone at all, but might also take a chunk out of your leg, and so better to try elsewhere.

As an activist, I work busily at legal, social, and physical things that try to keep all women safe all the time. But in these moments, my focus narrows to this femme, this street, this time, protecting her as best I can, not walking back and forth in front of the fence and growling, just slowly raising my big head.

So I walk differently. I pay less attention to avoiding other passersby, and let them avoid me. I pay more attention to steering my femme companion away from puddles and trash, and to seeing which gazes from oncoming pedestrians carry with them something I need to answer. I reply with a gaze I have practiced in front of a mirror for hours, honed with much use, one that clearly communicates that I have noted this person's interest in the femme I'm with, and that this is my yard, thank you. As complicated as it is, as much as I understand that it is not my most attractive behavior—I do it anyway. I do it out of habit, remembering every time a woman has looked beseechingly at me over the shoulder of some pawing jerk. I do it to give something back to these femmes who take such good care of me, in so many ways, in whatever small way I can. I do it because I spend enough time in the world of men to know what matters in those moments and how little it sometimes has to do with courtesy or kindness or equality.

I have full faith in the abilities of the estimable femmes in my life to kick ass and take names if necessary and appropriate. This is entirely separate from the theoretical feminist issues at work, and not to diminish in any way their own power. Please understand: what I hope I am doing, what I want to do, is to stand up straight, and use this size, this gender, this stride that cause me so much trouble some days—that which femmes nurture and love even when I hate and curse it—to protect them. On the page, in the classroom, I am trying to instill a feminist consciousness in everyone I can, but on the sidewalks I am keeping an eye on everyone my colleagues and I haven't gotten to yet.

WRESTLING

I bang my body against another butch's with unutterable joy. After a lifetime of being told to sit quietly, sit with my knees together, walk softly, not run, not play rough, not make noise, keep my body separate and my eyes down, it feels, even all these years later, like an act of revolution every time I walk up lightly, let my weight settle, and collide in the slowest possible motions with hir. I am glad for the solidness, glad to move with and against hir without having to worry about bowling hir over. Or, if I do, I can tug hir up from the ground with an apology full of good humor. That's if I can't catch hir before ze falls.

When the weather's nice and I am in some grass someplace with the butches and other transmasculine things I love, it seems that some wrestling always breaks out. Someone pounces on the unsuspecting, sleeping in the sun. Or the trading of pokes in the ribs escalates into grappling on the lawn, and everyone cheers and laughs and watches or piles on. Or a hug from behind morphs into someone trying to toss someone else over hir shoulder, slow-motion and full of the fond cushioning gestures we use when we don't want to hurt someone; we pull them down on top of us so we can absorb the impact and break the fall. If that seems like a metaphor for the way the best of butches operate in the world, I don't think it's an accident.

Always grappling, testing strength against strength, sometimes struggling for position, and sometimes just banging bodies for the animal pleasure of touch that is denied to us in other ways. It makes me think about the culture of football, about how lying prone along another man's back, patting his ass, holding him in a full-body hug—all things that are denied to men in the heterosexual matrix in which we live—are acceptable within that context. The pack-animal needs to lie down in a warm pile with others of our kind, safer together against predators and weather. Someone once said that a dog alone is only half a dog, and that seems just as right to me when talking about masculinely gendered people. A man alone may also be only half a man, and if men gravitate toward fraternities and sports teams and the military and their bowling leagues, I'd put my money on that as why.

Some men play pickup games of whatever sport for as long as their knees hold out, leaning on each other in the paint on schoolyard basketball courts and sliding into second on a squeeze play. Volumes have been written about homoeroticism in football, about the masculine imperative in American culture to keep one's body away from those of other men for fear of a gay panic. There seems no doubt that the intrinsic homophobia of manness in our culture keeps men apart no matter what their sexual orientation may in fact be. But I think the pile-on culture of men's athletic endeavors is less repressed homosexuality and more repressed needs of other kinds, about the hunger for contact, for physical touch, for the warmth and comfort of the pack.

At boarding school, I played snow football with the boys before brunch and then sometimes again before dinner every time we'd get a good snow on a weekend: a slipping, shouting, full contact version cushioned by fresh snow and the resilience of seventeen-year-old bodies. I remember how crazy screaming good it felt to be released for the first time from the strictures of girl socialization in my body, freed to crash into my peers, to use the bulk of my body as a weapon. To be prized for it, to get picked near the beginning of team choosing for the first time in my life; to be a valuable commodity for my absolute willingness to fling myself bodily at a windmill of arms and legs.

I didn't care if I got hurt, and even if I did, I never felt it until the next morning, when the adrenaline had receded and my muscles had warmed up enough to notice how many times I had been kicked with snow boots the previous day. No one ever hobbled as happily as I did to the dining hall for a big glass of juice to go with my handful of ibuprofen and then right back out onto the field. If I was only going to have a few opportunities to do this a year, I wasn't missing any of them on account of a little soreness in my shoulders. And back, and neck, and arms, and legs. It just felt so good, I kept trying to explain to my completely baffled roommates, one of whom had to pick my toothbrush up off the floor after an especially brutal game because I couldn't bend far enough to reach it.

I don't know if it felt so good because I am predisposed, barrel-bodied and broad-beamed, to seek that kind of contact, or if it was the sense of having it after being denied that made it so marvelous. I do know that, in my most exuberant moods, it is all I can do not to hip check everyone I see, not to leap upon my beloved Nicole or pull her down on me, not to knock my friends down with the sheer joy of being alive and in this body that lets me have this kind of pleasure. I do know that when I worked all day with elite male student-athletes at a Division I university, I got knocked into the cinderblock walls by the excessively enthusiastic greeting of my puppylike charges at least once a day, and I was always glad for it. It meant not only that they were engaging with me on the kind of fond level that it can be difficult to reach with students, but also that they were honoring the solidness of my butch body as a mass equal to their force. (I should add that knocking someone into the wall was more or less the point; it was not in any way a sign of weakness that I couldn't stand my ground.)

I know that when a group of butches are together on a sunny day, the odds of wrestling breaking out are high. It's such a pleasure; the sweetness of impact a gift of trust and also an honor of my strength, the strength girls are not supposed to have. Like the ties girls are not supposed to wear and the women girls are not supposed to woo and the boots girls are not supposed to fit into and every other part of it. And a pleasure in that way that pack animals call to one another, that like calls to like, skin calls to skin.

Exactly the way one teaches an abused dog to play, by barreling into them in the slowest possible motion, we learn to play with one another. We learn to take a threatening motion and cut it down to size with a big grin and the promise of our own broad chests to land on. We learn that we can test our strength in a place in which there are no negative consequences for failure; we grapple for position here without fear of danger. And we roll around on the grass in the warm sun and revel in getting to do it, in being at home in a safe place with our own kind, between battles, not losing the chance to train for the next one, but also not losing the moment to play with hearts full of joy.

BEING A BUTCH WITH YOUNG MEN

For one reason and another, I have chosen a number of jobs that have brought me into contact with boys and young men of the variety that used to be known as "troubled," but are now more often identified as "at-risk." These jobs include working in a prison teaching theater and creative writing, teaching study skills to collegiate athletes, making theater with disaffected inner-city teenaged boys, and so on. I started doing it in college when one of my community-service projects was working at an afterschool arts program and I ended up—by some magic of the Universe—with a little gang of boys in my charge, aged seven to twelve, who were pretty uniformly uninterested in theater, the program, and me, in that order. But they had burned through a couple of other volunteers in quick succession, and I was well known for being hardy, and so they got bucked over to me with the instruction that I was to try to keep them together and alive and from damaging children or property. If I was able to teach them anything about anything creative at all that would also be fine, but clearly not my first priority.

To everyone's great surprise, including mine, I had no particular problems with them at all. They were a little rowdy, and the first few days consisted of an unending series of tests to see just exactly how gullible I was, but then we settled in fine, even well enough to put together a couple of little skits for the end-of-the-semester talent show. Everyone was sort of amazed, and I felt quietly pleased. Later, in my community service evaluation, I read with some surprise that I had done powerful antisexism work, as evidenced by the fact that my charges, who were apparently rude, crude, and inappropriate to each of their previous female counselors, had none of those words for me. The logical conclusion drawn by the director was that I had somehow worked my upscale private college women's studies juju magic on them and fixed their wagons, but the truth was that we'd never talked about sexism, they hadn't behaved in any fashion that made it necessary, and I thought at the time that perhaps it had something to do with the fact that I was hardly a girl at all, anyway.

This kept happening to me. I would go into situations where traditionally man- or woman-gendered instructors were having a really hard time working with some young male students, and I had very few problems. People I worked with would ask me what I was doing to keep the guys either from harassing me as a woman, as they were doing with the female counselors, or playing my-dick-is-bigger-so-you-can't-tell-me-what-to-do, as they were doing with the male counselors, and I really had just absolutely no idea.

I shrugged my shoulders; I said, "I'm just talking to them"; I said, "We seem to do okay," and the general consensus was that I must be some sort of modern miracle of pedagogy, which I didn't really believe but also didn't, I must sheepishly confess, do a great deal to discourage. I was still trying to puzzle it out, still trying to identify what it was about my teaching style that made these young, at-risk male students—ranging from ADD victims of over-schooling to genuine convicted felons—pretty uniformly give me a pass on a wide variety of unsavory behaviors that they had unleashed without sympathy on other counselors and instructors.

The answer came while reading *Nearly Roadkill* by Kate Bornstein and Caitlin Sullivan. It's an erotic Internet adventure novel, and therefore the exact place I expected to find the answer to this question. In the book, one of the characters introduces the concept of traction: how in terms of sexual desire we see or experience what gender or other identity our partner or partners are embodying and then we push off of that, or against it; that it gives a kind of erotic traction, a place to play.

Upon reading that, I suddenly understood that my students had been derailed in their usual misbehavior because I'd slid in under their radar in my transgressively gendered way. No traction. If I had presented a recognizably feminine gender, they would have found themselves performing masculinity as it relates to "woman," an erotically charged response that called forth a known set of cues, ranging from sexually explicit comments to inappropriate remarks about women calculated to get a rise out of a female person. And if I had been recognizably man, they would have performed masculinity in a competitive way, making a point of pride out of not being "less than" me as men by refusing to cooperate or participate in activities. But by being neither a sexual object nor a competitive object, I short-circuited their usual modes of behavior and they had to relate to me as an individual, outside their paradigms. It was a little slice of completely undeserved grace.

As I began to understand where the lines were drawn in terms of previous, programmed responses, both to gender (because that was the one that led the way for me), and to any number of other things, I could see my way around them, in much the same way that formulaic action films have portrayed those few puffs of baby powder or cigarette smoke that will reveal the crisscrossing red beams of a complicated alarm system. In this movie, my gender was the revealing agent; it showed me all of the places that were defended, so that I could pick carefully among them and come out with the prize—in this case, getting students to listen to me.

Once I understood this, I started using it to my advantage: I would volunteer to work with the sort of students that responded best to my butch self, started looking for ways to change minds about carefully selected things, sneaking them new bits of information with no traction behind them so that they could take root without interference. We would talk about things like rape and sexual assault, homophobia, feminism, gender roles, and the interrelatedness of all forms of oppression.

I said things about gender, about sex, about violence into their silences that sometimes made the silences last for hours, even for guys who blasted gangsta rap and got their spending money from drug dealers back home. And they started to say things back to me, started to let me see parts of the interior landscapes of their gender, all full of caves and mines and dark places where monsters dwelled. Suddenly I was taken as a confidant into a whole new world, one that I understood instinctively from my experiences with compulsory femininity as a child.

I had resisted that femininity from a place of great privilege, from a sense of my parents' love and willingness to expend a lot of money and energy to keep me safe; and also with the sense of possibility that comes with white skin and an expensive education and plenty of chances to imagine myself into the world as someone more like Janet Reno than Karen Hughes. But they had so many fewer options, and even fewer role models than that: they looked at the boys and men of their experience who had been able to "make something of themselves" and sought to emulate them just as fervently as the communities into which they were born desired to shape them in that image.

It started to become clear to me that they had been unremittingly gendered from birth to behave in the ways that they did, that the behaviors about which we disagreed were as much a part of their culturally defined manhoods as their penises, and that leaving them behind seemed almost-but-not-quite as horrifying. This masculinity, this way of manhood, was the only hope they could see. They had been trained to be disdainful of, even fearful of, femininity in any form; the ability to put the most distance between themselves and any shred of it was a paramount issue in their survival and success.

The shaming that they had been subjected to as small boys whenever they displayed any characteristic thought to be feminine had grown in them into a particularly bitter anger. We talked about how much masculinity was enough, and the ways in which confidence could be separated from the performance of "manliness." Over and over, as though it were a prayer, I told a story my father had told me as a kid:

NFL Hall of Famer Rosie Grier, the legendary, gigantic, supremely talented defensive lineman for the Los Angeles Rams, had the habit of needlepointing. He said it relaxed him, and he enjoyed it. One night he was being interviewed, and toward the end the interviewer looked at him and said, "So, Rosie, listen. Don't the guys, you know, tease you about doing *needlepoint*?" And Rosie Grier, in a moment of great grace, turned his mammoth head to face the interviewer, and the camera pulled back to show his body, his enormous powerful body at rest in the chair with such quiet containment and he said:

"No."

BREASTS

There are few things in my universe more complicated, more complex, more dependent on context than breasts. Every time I think I have reached a place of conclusion about them, some further question asserts itself and I am once again hopelessly mired in the muck, trying to generalize about something about which one ought not generalize. I think that I have formulated a thesis, and then it turns out to have more holes than my favorite socks. There is nothing I can say about breasts from A Butch Standpoint, no way I can make even one statement about butches and breasts that I feel confident is going to be almost always true, except: butches recognize breasts on sight. There. Now I feel better.

An earlier draft of this essay flowed from the following thesis: Breasts, for butches, fall into that category of things known as "lovely for you, not acceptable for me." I was thinking about those things, things like feelings and sundresses, those things that the stereotype of butch praises or admires in others but does not have a natural affinity for in hirself. But after the flurry of typing came the inevitable flurry of deleting as I thought about the butches I know who do like their breasts (and also those who like feelings, and those who like sundresses, and they are not always the same butches, for the record). The way their breasts can be made to feel if not the way they look, or sometimes both. And my enormous desire not to leave them, or any butch, feeling shamed for nonnormative behavior. We have enough of *that* as it is. So that thesis was right out.

The further problem, of course, is that any thesis requires

some stillness of thought, and mine is not. I look down at my own breasts, rounded and small compared to my barrel-chested frame, and the first thing I remember is getting the tattoo over my heart. The artist, a lithe and talented man with stylized waves lapping over his clavicles, silently tried a variety of yogic positions to achieve the requisite tautness of skin without having to actually touch my breast. Finally, tentatively, he indicated it with the slightest motion of his tattoo needle and explained his problem.

"Grab hold," I said, "I'm not delicate." He did with the slightest of shrugs, and the mark emerged perfect from his confident ministrations, the entire tattoo created with my left breast held firmly in his hand as though it were being prepared for cooking. Only later did I realize that he wasn't afraid of hurting me, he was afraid to touch what he perceived as my girl parts in such a proprietary way, without first ascertaining my consent. I imagine that my reply must have been somewhat confusing, but by then I wasn't thinking about that. The hard part, unmasking what gets seen as my female body, was over. I was deep into the anticipation of the ink I had been dreaming about for a year. There was no question that he could do whatever was needful to make it happen.

The scene jumps. I had a lover once, a transguy, who was full of plans to have top surgery when I met him. After six months he told me that he was thinking twice about it because he had discovered in the intervening time that he really liked the sensation of his nipples, which he had rarely allowed to be touched. He didn't want to lose it. He said that because I had breasts and was not a woman, it felt somehow acceptable to enjoy it when I touched him in those ways. It was somehow all right, because the equivalency in our shapes also had congruency, and that made it safe for him. Complicated a thought as that is, I understand it; it feels metaphysically different to be touched by someone whose map of the body has the same markings on it, the same legend.

A lover once cupped my breast in her hand, and her own almost identical breast in her other hand and said, fondly, "Same." I smiled as best I could, but I knew it was wrong. She was only seeing the physical equivalency of the two heaps of flesh, and not the incongruent relationships we had with them. I loved my breasts for the possibilities of great pleasure they carried, but hated them for marking me as a woman in bigendered society, a woman I never felt like and still don't. She treasured the curves of her shape; the skim of fabric over her breasts was something she displayed with pleasure and a sureness of their role in her attractiveness. I treasured them too, for many reasons, not the least of which was: they weren't mine.

My breasts were, are, a thing to be hidden. Even as I write this, if I still myself for a minute, I can feel the edges of a binder digging into the softness of my sides and compressing my ribcage just slightly, leaving me unable to draw a full breath. I know how thick the fabric of a T-shirt must be to retain its shape over my chest and not cling to my bound breasts, and what structure of dress shirt best makes the starched fabric fall from my shoulder to my belt with the least hint of the underlying topography. I have the advantage of being a large-framed person, and I have studied intensively the movements of men who are shaped like me—the ones who are fat and somewhat squashy and have what I affectionately refer to as "fat boy tits," and the ones who are fat but strongly muscled and have a development of pectoral muscle with a layer of fat over them that closely resembles what my bound chest looks like under most shirts.

I see how they hold their upper bodies slightly stiff, how the associated development of their latissimus dorsi from the same work that bulks their pecs makes them just slightly musclebound, makes their elbows stand just a bit away from their sides. I mimic it, all the while grateful for the broad shoulders and barrel chest I inherited from my father that give the whole arrangement a certain physiological legitimacy to the glances of passersby. If I want to pass as male, or at least if I want my gender to be a moment of complication, then genetics and good movement-training are on my side; I can make it look good. Good, for this moment, meaning masculine.

Butches and the binding of our breasts have a long and complicated history. Leslie Feinberg's classic, beautiful novel *Stone Butch Blues* mentions early on Butch Al being brought back to a holding cell after a raid, saying "her binder was gone, leaving her large breasts free." Questioning butches of the era, I learned that—then as now—many butches bound their breasts with Ace bandages or other tension-style bandages, and specifically that in the era before sports bras, most women's undergarments were designed to display, rather than disguise, breasts.

The Ace bandage was the only alternative to the push-up bra, the conical bra, and the demi-cup lace bra, and butches used them to make their chests as flat as they could, to hide the lines of their breasts under their work clothes and finery alike. Though high-density sports bras (some of which are made and marketed especially for those creatures with breasts, of whatever sex, who would rather not have them) are now more common for this purpose, there are many butches who cannot bear to wear an item that resembles a bra in any way and so contort ourselves daily in our mirrors, wrapping ourselves tight and breathless in rolls of bandage. The symbolism of bandaging this complicated and painful part of ourselves that includes our hearts is not lost on any of us.

The first time I ever saw a butch bind her breasts was on stage. Peggy Shaw, my teacher and mentor, performed a show called *You're Just Like Your Father*, which opened with her sitting still in a chair downstage right, in a puddle of light, wearing nothing but a pair of boxer shorts and a long Ace bandage draped around her neck. As she began to speak she stood and started to wrap herself, expertly, creating a binding in minutes that held without a wrinkle until the show ended. Peggy made a connection between binding her breasts and wrapping her hands in boxing wraps; this was what one did before battle, to protect one's self (and it is the Self, absolutely, that binding protects for many butches). Seeing this performance for the first time, I was deeply uncomfortable watching what was happening onstage. Her naked chest was not troublesome, and neither was her bound one, but observing the awkward and ungainly process of binding seemed like an intrusion, as though the decent thing for all of us would have been to close our eyes or avert our gazes instead of watching, fascinated, while this most intimate transformation took place.

Every time I have seen anyone bind hir breasts since, I cannot help but be reminded of Peggy, tall and handsome with the gravel of South Boston still in her throat, talking about protection while binding her breasts. Every time, I am struck with the same feeling of having been caught and shown something I simultaneously cannot take my eyes from and would rather not see. And when I sometimes, for advanced classes of gender studies, give a performance/lecture called "Body Politics," in which I discuss with the class five aspects of the performance of gender on the body—dress, grooming, body posture, referent of gaze, and body position in relation to others—and with their help, demonstrate the spectrum of these things, I take up the other side of the experience.

The part about dress, saved for last, requires me to take off my masculine attire, to remove my gender to "reveal" my sex. Unbinding my breasts from the Ace bandage I use just for the occasion is never, ever as difficult as rebinding with all of them watching, fascinated. By this time all the students have worked it out that I have breasts under there, so showing them, much like in the tattoo artist's chair, is not the difficult part. Their existence is known, and the gendered issues that come with them dealt with; I do not mind such revelations. But I watch to see who is delighted, who is disgusted, and who is taking careful notes on how it's done.

Allowing one's breasts to be seen, however, is not the same thing as allowing them to be touched. My intimate life with butches and other transmasculine things has shown me that the dizzying variety of human sexuality sometimes becomes even more specific when navigating the minefields of body dysphoria. I said once in a conference session, only half-kidding, that the first question I asked trans lovers when it became clear that sex was imminent was "What can I touch, and what do you call it?"

I am used to being told, by now, that I can touch a butch's breasts but may not call them that, or may not call them anything; that I can put my palms flat against them but not cup my hands, or squeeze; that I can work hir nipples with my hands but not my mouth. Or vice versa. But I do not touch a masculinely gendered, assigned-female person's breasts without express permission. I want for them to feel as desirable as I think they are, and I know from my own experience that the wrong touch, the wrong body memory, can send even the most formerly willing partner through the looking glass and into a place in which being sexual is the last thing on hir mind. I tread carefully. I take my time. I check in, murmuring "Is this okay?" even if I have been told that it is; I want to make sure I am getting it right from the outset. I want to give my butch lovers pleasure without the sense of danger that being naked in front of another can bring.

Of course, I also worry about this. I worry that my assumption that this is a delicate and dangerous thing adds to the mythology of butches who must, who always, hate everything about their breasts. I wonder whether my gentle, loving questioning strikes anyone as being strange in its solicitousness. I am afraid that it may make some butch wonder if maybe ze is not supposed to like that.

I am afraid that my hands, stroking ribs and backs and the precious curves of bellies, across strong shoulders and tattooed biceps but avoiding breasts until I can find the moment to ask, might make some handsome butch feel shamed to have breasts, or think that I do not find them attractive or wish they were not there.

Did I say it was a complex issue?

And there's no ending, really. There is no final statement to make on the subject of breasts, no conclusion to draw, no way to say anything for sure except that when it comes to breasts, nothing is simple. When it comes to breasts, gender and truth and trust and skin complicate one another in a thousand directions, beautiful and grotesque, comforting and dangerous, charmed and strange. Then again, the same could be said of butches.

WHY I'M NOT A NICE YOUNG MAN (YET)

I've read my Kessler and McKenna, my Carol Gilligan, my Kate Bornstein, not to mention my Viola Spolin and David Mamet and others of that theatrical ilk, and I understand gender attribution. I know what things mean male, or female, to people who are gendered and socialized in this country, under the none-too-benevolent tutelage of Standard American Television Gender. For the most part, I can pass; I can get the gender attribution that I want if I care about which I get. It makes my parents a little twitchy when waitstaff call me sir, for sure, and it seems a little unsafe sometimes to be a big freakshow of a gender-fucking thing some of the places I go, so I go for Big Dude instead, and that works nicely.

I can think about it and adjust my gender cues accordingly: my voice, for example, the way I use my hands, hold my head, sit, stand, take up space, meet people's eyes. In most public circumstances, though, my big body and walk and stance make people peg me as man, or at least masculine, and I'm fine about it. Maybe even glad.

Sir, you see, gets better service. Sir gets points for saying please and thank you, and I was raised to understand "May I please," as a single word, to be employed frequently. Sir makes straight-girl waitresses of a certain age flirt and preen when they come past our table. Sir is allowed to walk right into the repair bay; Sir gets to walk back to the car at night without worrying much about who's in the shadows; Sir raises his chin at the bartender and gets another drink, just like that. Sir gets to browse unmolested among the racks at stores, gets to avoid the perfume guerillas with a curt shake of the head; Sir is believed when he says he knows his shoe size, oil weight, preferred cut of steak, way back to the main road from here. Sir is always next when there are two people waiting, and Sir is a gentleman of the highest order if he defers his place to a waiting woman. Sir is allowed to have seconds without comment.

But there's more. The same characteristics, the same behaviors that are fine for Sir are troublesome if I'm Ma'am. When I'm a Sir, I'm a big guy, and when I'm Ma'am, I'm indecently fat. When Sir is fat and needs a seatbelt extension on an airplane, no one ever suggests that he ought to have bought two seats or gives him a look of barely veiled disgust. When Sir orders a Coke, he gets one.

When Ma'am orders a Coke, half the time Diet Coke arrives with a lemon floating accusatorily in it. This is perhaps my least favorite thing about gender. When Sir offers to get a lady's bag down from the overhead compartment, or offers her his arm getting across the street, or carries a giant potted plant out from the store, he gets a nice pat on the hand. If Ma'am tries, she gets looked at a little funny.

Sir never gets to hold strangers' babies, which Ma'am often does. Both are hopelessly sweet on kids and dogs. But otherwise, the public butch Sir has the better end of the deal.

Some days this is enough to make me want to take hormones and have surgeries. Some days the ease, the smooth grace of being a Nice Young Man, seems so appealing that I want to embody it all the time, unquestionably and unmistakably. I want my father's five o'clock shadow to spread across my face, and for my hips and tits to run away together to parts unknown, and my voice to come down the last half octave I need to get all the way to tenor, even if I haven't had a cigarette. I could be Sir all the time, I could always get my salad with extra dressing and always have an empty seat next to me on the bus until all the ones by women were taken. I could kiss my beloved on any street corner in the Western world and never even get looked at askance. I could do ally work as a feminist and a homophile, say revolutionary things at conferences and bowling alley bars and anyplace else and never get discounted as another one of those strident whatevers.

But Sir is a man, and I am a butch. I am willing to be a man for a while, when it's convenient or safe or pleasant, but inevitably I want to be able to coo inanely at little children and not have their mothers come and grab them away. I want to go and see my mechanic and confess without an ounce of shame that something is the matter and I haven't the faintest idea what it might be. I want to be seen in the world as safe instead of strong, I want to hold hands and cry. I want to order girly blender drinks all summer long and use a restroom that has a passing chance of some remote acquaintance with cleaning products in its recent past, and perhaps most of all I want to be queer, visibly queer, several bubbles off gender and tilting fast. I want the outlaw I am to get a public hearing, a public viewing, and to have a chance to speak for hirself.

As much as my masculinity is comfortable on me, as much as there are moments when being a man is convenient or satisfying, I have invested a lot of time and energy in making the world a safer place for queers and I am not ready to be finished with that work yet. Going out in the world as a masculinely gendered, female-bodied person, as a butch, creates a kind of queer visibility that I could never approach as Sir.

More than that, though, more than all of those things, I like being able to choose. I like being able to put my gender on with my clothes in the morning, take it off at night, change it during the day, shift my voice and hands between the mechanic and the art supply store and have my public face just the way I want it. There is an ineffable comfort in having a body that is as much a shapeshifter as my brain is, a gender that leaves me so many options for education and helping and flirting—my favorite things. And though I am sheepish about wanting something so self-serving, I also want to play. I want to have my way with gender before it has its way with me, lead it around by the shorthairs, tease it, and then do—and have—exactly what I want anyway, each and every time.

COCKS

I know that this can be used as a weapon, and every time I take it in hand I remember that. I remember that it has been used that way against me, against you, against so many of the people I know—it, or an analogue of it, some tool used to open what does not wish opening—and I keep that knowledge fresh in my body when I come to you wearing it. Every time is like introducing a dog-fearing child to my own dog. I hold it firmly and away, giving you time to see it, to see my face, to decide all for yourself in this moment after the unveiling whether it is what you really want, whether you can greet it or need it to be taken away.

I turn it into a play, a little moment of traction within our intimacy. I make you show me your desire right here. But not to shame you, never that; I love your desire. It's the only thing I want right now. I am just marking with my body and this tool the space between what I want and what you want, making sure they are the same thing.

My cock is rubber, insensate, it does not need or want any-thing on its own and that's what I like about it. I know people who can come from fucking this way, the bases of their cocks pounding into them until they come into their partners, and I know people who lament that this is not the case for them. I do not lament it. I am glad to be able to be fully focused on you when we do this, on your pleasure, on your breath and eyes and skin under my hands. I am glad to be able to go on as long as it suits you, and to stop when you're finished. Not being distracted by my own immediate need is part of my pleasure. It helps me to keep my eyes open, my movements calculated to please you. I am sure that there are those who can keep track of all of that and still fuck to their own climax, but I am not one of them. Just the sight of you wrapped around my cock nearly undoes me.

When I take young butches and boys shopping for their first dicks, they always want the biggest one. Size matters, they know, and they want something big enough to make men keep their distance and women flush and giggle and others nod knowingly. They reach, half-glazed, for the Magnum or the Johnny Max or the Jeff Stryker model with the squeezable balls, imagining the power of it. Imagining that a dick gives them any power at all, they hold the outsize things to their crotches and mime stroking them. I remember that the first thing I did with my first dick and harness was go home and look at myself in the mirror. It felt like power to me then.

But the power of it, I tell them, isn't yours, and once you forget that, you run the risk of crossing lines no honorable person would cross. Any penetration is a grace offered to you by the person you're inside; it is an intimate way of inclusion, a gift. No matter how hard or rough the fuck, no matter who is the top or bottom or anything else, no matter the genders of the participants, this is a world in which opening one's self to someone else is always somewhere on the continuum between a gesture of welcome and an office of trust, and you should be grateful.

I have never come out of someone's body without thanking them for the privilege, and even when my lovers have scoffed at me or insisted that I am the one who deserves thanks, I say it anyway. I am humbled and grateful. I know, too, that there are few better moments in which to make someone feel precious, and I hate to lose the opportunity.

That said, there is such joy in that first cock, in that first possibility of being able to lie with the object of your affection the way you have imagined it (if you have imagined it this way, which not all butches do). And in that joy there is undeniably a different kind of power, a sense of agency, a feeling of being able to make yourself visible on the landscape of sexuality in a whole new way.

It didn't even take a dick for me; I strutted around in my brand-new black boxer briefs like a cross between a bantam rooster and a porn star, playing the most explicit tracks in my CD collection and checking myself in the mirror to see how I looked while grinding (the answer, in case you had even a moment's doubt, was: ridiculous). So having the sudden pleasure of being ready for the kind of sex you dream of can be a fierce kind of joy, the kind one takes in any desirable but dangerous new toy, like a brand-new three-bladed jackknife. Are you going to run out and immediately start poking and hacking at things? Yes. Are you going to get hurt that way? Almost certainly. Are you going to run back out as soon as you're half-healed and continue playing in a decidedly unauthorized fashion? Hell, yes. The thing to be sure of, I always try to say, is that you don't hurt anyone else with this particular new toy.

I am not sure I know anyone who has actually managed not to, of course, with even the best of intentions. Myself included. But I hope that saying these things will help the less sensitive become more so, and the more sensitive avoid doing things that will tear them up inside. I truly hope so. But the tools we use on our own and others' flesh are always a delicate proposition, and there's really no way to stay entirely clear of mistakes; the best we can hope for is that they will be small ones and that we will recognize them quickly so we may begin to make amends. What else is there to do?

I have a collection of cocks now, accumulated sometimes for the taste of my partners and sometimes out of my own want of change. I refer to them with a certain self-mocking amusement as my (not so) little overcompensation, and I encourage my partners to take their choice of sizes, but it is true that there is a default item, the one I think of and wear as my cock, not as my plastic sex-toy attachment.

I am always happy to swap out, but that one feels comfortable and natural in a way that none of the others quite do; I always feel like Goldilocks, but there really is one that's just right. The mine-ness of it may be in the physics, in the length and shape and weight that make it so much easier than any of the others to control, or it may be a process of accretion: the accumulated pleasures it and I have had with the people who have graced me so, building up in layers and making it (and me) feel more sure. It shows the signs of use and wear, for sure, and I wonder what I will feel when I have to retire it for its nearly identical replacement. I wonder how long it will take to feel like mine, whether the difference will be palpable to anyone I might come to with it as it seems to be now; though I always offer to change sizes to suit, I am usually refused with identical answers.

"No," my partners have said. "I want *yours*, I want your cock inside me."

They're all mine and all not-mine, I want to answer. I bought them all for cash and carried them away in bags. I may have more skill or practice with this one, but the attention and affection and great gratitude I bring to any moment in which I use it is what's really mine. That's what you feel under me, or astride, or however it works out; that's what I am offering. I am offering my desire to balance my female body with this item of our pleasure, and my empathy as a person who has been penetrated myself, sometimes with great love and sometimes with annihilating violence. None of them will give you more or less of me.

But treat it gently nonetheless. That's what I don't say. This is the last thing, the last and most difficult truth of my cock, for me. It is a difficult thing, some days, to come to you knowing that I'm not equipped by birthright with everything it takes to please you. There has to be the purchasing and trying out, the fumbling with straps and the groping after snaps, the telltale marks of my lack angry on my skin afterward where straps or buckles fastened tight have dug into my tender flesh. If I could stand it, I would ask you to soothe and pleasure those hurt places with your mouth as wonderfully as you take my cock in your mouth while we're fucking.

As it is, if you could just not laugh, I would be grateful. The extra touches like keeping it warm against your body afterward, just as though it could feel the cold, and licking underneath the head as though it were an especially sensitive spot, are very nice, and I adore you for them. The cock, as I said, is rubber, insensate, which I am glad of most days, and on some level your tender attentions to it are ridiculous. But I am not insensate, and your choice to treat what I cannot help but see as broken as though it were whole is another great gift, another moment of grace, so unexpected and so welcome.

BORDER WARS

"You cannot piss in a cup or pull a sword from a stone or any-thing else in order to tell if you're trans or not. You are if you want to be. You're not if you don't."

This is what I say. No one listens.

"Look. I define transgendered literally; it's a way of crossing. Crossing into a different gender. Not the opposite, there are so *many*, just a different one. Or crossing out of the gender that the-oretically goes, in that there heterosexual matrix we keep talking about, with your biological sex.

"Being a transsexual is a different animal. That's a matter of medical things or the intention of medical things, changing your *sex*, you know? The sex parts: genitals, reproductive organs, hor-mones, secondary sexual characteristics. Or living full-time as a person of a certain culturally aligned sex and gender, whether you do medical things or not, because some people can't and it isn't fair to punish that. So them, too. But transgendered is wide open. And butch is a nonnormative gender, yes? We can agree on that, anyway? So if you want to claim transgendered, great as far as I'm concerned."

People sigh at me. They roll their eyes, They shake their heads. They want me to make a ruling, they want me to tell them if they can call themselves transgendered, or, alternately, if they can still call themselves butch. As though I somehow have the power to confer or deny whatever label they want, or as though I can be relied upon to make an impartial decision in the case of an argument, whether it is internal or among individuals.

They want to know what disclaimer they should use, how to explain the complexities of gender to beginners so that they will understand that butch can be, but isn't always, a trans identity. They say this even as they, the trans things themselves, presumably the world experts on their own identities, stand in front of me, hoping that I will clarify.

"All I can tell you is what I see," I insist, and they reply:

"Okay, tell me that."

All right. On the one hand I see butch as a historical construct, butch as a way of gender that is separate from both man and woman, and every other gender. I see it as a deviant gender, a *trans*gender, a way of being gendered that is neither normative nor recognized as such either culturally or sociologically. Often, but not always, a female masculinity; occasionally also a man's way of being a man that is so queerly consonant with the best of considered masculinity that ze steps out of the gender of man. But transgressive, nonetheless.

In real terms, in its most common, most delicious, female masculinity incarnation, butch looks queer. Queer in the old way: queer as in different, peculiar to the normative eye. It looks like a way of being in the world that does not conform to the standard cultural gender binary. Strictly in terms of the text of the body that is available to the public gaze, butch is a place of difference, and butches have long struggled with that and chosen to honor one another for it, for that exact way of deviance that the culture finds abhorrent, or at least confusing.

When femmes talk to me about butches, that visible way of difference is one of the things they report liking about butches. When butches talk to me about butches, they speak with great love of the character created in a person who lives outside the protection of invisibility, of the "normal," someone who is forced to make new ways of living correctly in hir gender. We know what the cultural ideals of woman and man are, much as we may disagree with them. The cultural ideals of butch are so much newer, so much more nebulous, and yet we seem to know when it's being done well. When people speak admiringly of a butch, what I see is someone who has taken on the best gendered characteristics of both woman and man, left a lot of the stuff born of misogyny and heterosexism behind, and walked forward into the world without apology.

(For the record, I believe that the same is true of femmes; the femmes who get the most admiration, the most approbation in the queer community in which I live seem to be the ones who cherry-pick exactly what of femininity they want, mix it with a hearty dash of traditionally masculine characteristics like sexual agency, stompy boots, assertiveness, fondness for power tools, and so on, and shake up a gendered cocktail that makes traditional unexamined cultural femininity look a little watery, a little pale.

This is what I see, as a longtime admirer of femmes in all their variations, but I freely acknowledge that I only see what any femme cares to show me, and it's really not for me to say. The last thing the femmes I love would appreciate out of me is for me to pretend to speak for them, which I could never do. Even if I could, I wouldn't, because Holy Reifying Femme Invisibility, Batbutch.)

I hear from butches that they are saddened by what they think of as Butch Flight, that people who once might have lived as butches are now living as men, and it makes them sad. They want back the visibly queer phalanx of butches, and they want the kick-ass women butches sometimes embodied. Feminism, they insist, is not being helped by the fact of women with masculine qualities decamping from Women's Space to the Old Boys Network. They're fearful that soon, masculine women like them will be a more or less extinct species. And they are grieving, some of them, that after being thrown out of the women's movement for being too male-identified they are now being ridiculed or having their identities questioned for being not male-identified enough.

I have heard a hundred versions of the same comment:

"If one more green-haired twenty-year-old who says [hir] gender is xylophone calls me *he* without even asking me what I prefer just because I have short hair and wear motorcycle boots, I am going to scream. Be a xylophone all you want, kid. But I'm a butch woman, and I am not a *he*."

And it is a difficult point to argue.

And then, I hear from FTMs, MTMs, transmen, trannyboys, transguys, and so on—pick your favorite or write in your own—who are deeply troubled by the idea of butches claiming trans identities. I hear them talk about how difficult it is for them to make the transition, to insist that people respect their choices and their genders, and how difficult it is to make their mothers call them *he* and *Jonathan*, when those same mothers are reading about young genderqueer butches who don't care what pronoun you use and cheerfully rename themselves with at least marginally gender-neutral things like *Cooper* and *Jaden*. They speak about how some days it feels like there is not enough distance in the world to put between themselves and the genderqueer community—not because they disapprove of genderqueers, but because they couldn't be more different and so few people seem to understand that. These men share how hard it is to find love or even intimate companionship with people who can see them in their genders and can lie down with them without making them ashamed of their bodies.

When I talk to people of whatever gender who love transmen, they tell me how brave their men and boys are to venture into a difficult and alien landscape with so little help. These people are fiercely, brilliantly proud of them for managing to keep their often-hated topographically female bodies alive long enough to nourish their precious minds and souls so that they could transition and live as men. They love transguys' burgeoning fur and warm, warm skin and they are glad to soothe themselves against it whenever they can.

Some FTMs feel disrespected when someone whose main commitment to gender change has been the purchase of a few neckties starts calling himself a transguy, as though their entire gender could really be summed up that way. Many transmen I have spoken with have given up a lot to re-embody themselves as men; in some cases nothing less than money, relationships, family, security, and any sense of home. They are deeply frustrated with butches who take on man-ness and masculinity when it suits them, but still go home for family holidays or to corporate jobs in women's clothes, where they are called she. These butches, the transmen say, want to eat their cake and have it too.

"I am tired of getting treated like some sort of superbutch, like an annex of the lesbian community, instead of like a man. Be a butch all you want, but I am a transman, and it is not the same thing."

It is an easy thing to understand, that feeling that after so much work and differentiation, so much sacrifice and desire, they are more or less just about a half step from where they started and that this is the fault of butches who identify as trans. If trans can encompass so many things, the argument goes, then what good is it? How does one mark one's self as substantially different?

"I actually transitioned," is the murmuring undercurrent I discern, "I deserve my *trans*, you get your own word." And again, it is a difficult point to argue.

Then there is another entire group of transmasculine folks, without a lot of overlap with the first group, who have transitioned with hormones or surgery or both, and still identify as butch. Or, some wonder if that's okay for them to do. They were raised as butch, they contend, they had that outsider experience and they want to preserve it in their identities. They have, they say, butch hearts, and they want to be recognized as men and also as butches, or as butches and also as men.

Yet they are tentative about publicly identifying as butch. Many feel as though they no longer deserve it, that they have, in fact, decamped and have given up their visas to that place. Some speak of themselves hesitantly as transmen of butch experience; they qualify and offer caveats; and when I ask them why, they tell me that it seems very complicated, that people think of butches as women and they don't want to be women, but also that butch as an identity seems to them to have a cultural place they don't feel entitled to. I wonder, are there also butches of trans experience?

Once I've spun the whole thing out as best I can understand it, faithfully reported what I have heard and understood, reminded whomever it is that I am sure I have made mistakes and that I apologize for them but I don't always know where they are, they always ask the same thing: "But what do *you* think?"

And I sigh.

What do I think? I think that all of these concerns and fears and angers and loves and all are completely valid and perfectly reasonable and utterly understandable. And I think that if we don't quit spending so much energy on fighting amongst ourselves, we are going to look up one day soon and find the Department of Homeland Security on our collective doorstep, confiscating our papers and banning us from travel or work for being security risks by virtue of being too confusing, one and all. Then we'll realize what a privilege it was to engage in border wars, when we had the leisure time for that. Before we ended up spending every scrap of energy on survival. That's what I think.

Fold it, iron it, and put it in your back pocket—not the one with your wallet, the other one. It can move from pocket to pocket for a few days, perhaps a week, before it needs to be pulled out, rinsed out, and ironed again. Just carrying it with you is not enough; it must be maintained in a state ready for use. Imagine the most fastidious femme thing you know putting it to her face, and let her be your guide.

WATCHING OUR FATHERS

We watch our fathers. If we're lucky at all, if they're any good at all, this is where we begin to learn, before we have any sense of what we're learning, or why, before they understand what we're watching for, we watch them.

I'm sitting on the counter in the steamy bathroom while he, wrapped tight in a towel, shaves carefully, dotting shaving cream onto my nose, tickling me with his shaving brush, making me giggle my little girl giggle, not knowing at first twenty years later why it is that I have no problem dampening my own brush, swirling it in the cake of soap in my shaving mug, and lathering up when some boys I know can't manage an even coat with canned foam.

Sitting with him on a Sunday afternoon on the living room floor, canvas spread out over the carpet so my mother doesn't have a fit, polishing all the shoes in the house: his own for work, my mother's, my tiny loafers. It's my job to brush the shoes, and I do it with vigor. It has been explained to me that the friction of the brush creates heat, creates the shine, and even though I know my father will take the brush from me at some point, and, with it in his massive hand, give each shoe a flurry of a dozen strokes across each toe, I can still be relied upon to brush the rest of the shoe well enough.

I go with him to the gentlemen's store when he shops, and I listen and watch while he tries on suits, considers ties, talks to me about color and weight, pattern and cut, while my little brother plays G.I. Joe on his belly under the suit racks when no one's looking. I help my father choose ties and match pocketsilks; we talk about the tassels on loafers. He indulges me because I am his daughter, his little girl, and little girls are supposed to be interested in soft and shiny fabrics, in colors that match and clash, and because he loves anything we can do together, but I am filing this information away. I am watching him as he selects the right color socks and discusses the break of his trouser legs across his instep. I march around the house later in his old suit jacket and shoes.

I watch him move the heavy stuff without betraying any outward sign of how heavy it is, except that his face gets so red I get scared. He picks up whatever needs to be picked up and moves it to wherever it needs to go and doesn't say a word about it. Only some years later, when I am inducted into Butch Local 139 and spend almost every summer weekend humping someone's entire life up and down two flights of stairs, do I realize how hard that is.

He does a little soft-shoe to get to the door in time to open it, which I learn. He has a motion of his head, a raise of his eyebrows that gets the check put right into his hand, so subtle that no one but an adoring daughter could notice it. He sends my mother first and puts his hand on the small of her back when they thread through an aisle or a tight spot; he holds his body firm when we dance and leads me in his frame so that I look like I know exactly what I'm doing, and I'm grateful for that. He scolds me to look at him, not at my feet, but I'm not looking at my feet, I'm looking at his, and at the angle of his elbow and the tilt of his hips. In my room later on that night and for weeks to follow, I hum the song we danced to and lead my imaginary partner around the room, suave and in control, my arms stiff and my hands soft—soft, just like they're supposed to be.

Now, when I go on a date, I have my father with me murmuring into my ears when I shine my shoes, shave away the bit of
scruff on my face. A man should have a close shave, I remember
him saying as he worked scalding water and a badger brush and
a double-blade razor across his face until his cheeks were velvet
smooth. I put on clean slacks or jeans and a nice structured-and-
placketed dress shirt with a lot of starch and a heavyworked Ital-
ian silk tie, and my shiny shoes, and we go out to dinner. I order
a dessert I don't want so my wife who can't make up her mind can
try mine too. Then we are dancing, and I'm clean and shiny and
I smell good and I take her in my arms and the DJ, who's my old
friend, puts on a slow one, and we set off across the floor, her safe
in my embrace, her hands soft in my hands, and she slides her
cool thumb across my palm, and I'm damn glad I paid attention.

BRIDAL REGISTRY

I did not exactly set out to be a Bride. I didn't set out to be a Groom, either. In much the same way that I have a wife but I am not a husband, I had a Bride but I was not a Groom. Not only that, but people kept asking me what I was, then, as though the union of souls could not continue until the taxonomy had been satisfied. I was clear that I was not a Bride. I was willing to be a Groom, but it didn't quite seem like the thing; I suggested that she was Beauty, and I was the Beast. Harlequin and Columbine, I offered, bird and bee, but the prevailing sentiment was that either I was a Bride or I was a Groom. I dug in and announced that I was a Bear, that I had chosen a Russian girl on purpose so that the Bride and the Bear would make cultural sense, and now, if I could please be excused from the conversation, I had yarmulkes to order.

That went more or less all right until the Bridal Registry.

What you want to avoid is gender confusion at the Bridal Registry desk. It's not the Wedding Registry, or the Spousal Registry, no matter what the forms may now read—it is a glorious bulwark of heteronormativity against the rising queer tides. They are really not prepared for gender nonconformity in the Bridal Registry area; it makes them suspicious and irritable and you start to get the sense that these are women who chose Bridal Registry work for a *reason*, so that they could surround themselves with none but the dewy newly affianced, heterosexuality rampant. And they do flock, make no mistake. This was still the Bridal Registry, and I was a Bride.

So there we were, sitting in fussy chairs in the white-and-gilt corner of the world that is the purview of cheerful Scottish Margaret, sensible from brogue to brogans and ready to initiate us into the wide and wonderful world of place settings. From a tiny drawer in her confection of a desk she produced a little stack of forms and started asking questions: Were we (and here, just the slightest proprietous pause) living together? We were. How long, please, and what had we amassed during that time? Did we entertain, cook much, cook extravagantly? Did we think of ourselves as formal, classic, contemporary, or rustic in style? Like thousands of Grooms before me, I sat silently while Nicole answered questions in the language of housewares. Though she seemed to have an instinctive understanding of my gender, perhaps confirmed by the way I spaced out slightly during a discussion of glassware, I had no idea what Margaret thought about my sex, and I wasn't really full of the desire to ask her, except that a somewhat delicate issue had to be broached: we needed to explain to Margaret that I needed to be listed as the Bride.

Bridal registries, you understand, are to facilitate gift-buying, and the practical sides of both Nicole and me realized that while my whole extended family and many of our family friends would be likely to use the registry to send engagement and wedding gifts, her comparatively small family, most of whom disapproved deeply of our wedding, were not likely to be sending us a couple of place settings of our chosen blue and white dinnerware. That was part one of the problem.

Part two, bridal registries are also ruthlessly gendered: you use a little touch-screen kiosk to type in the name of either the Bride or the Groom, and it shows the registry. If you type a name filed under Groom in a space for a Bride, it does not suggest to you that "There is no Bride by that name but perhaps you meant Groom?" It blinks dumbly at you and says: No Match Located. I have since learned that this is not the case at Macy's, where some forward-thinking powers-that-be revamped the system years ago to be a Spouse 1/Spouse 2 arrangement, with all names cross-referenced to all categories. We, however, did not register at Macy's. Putting the issue of my family doing the gifting together with the Bride/Groom issue forced a question: how on earth were we going to convince my relatives to type my name in as a Groom?

Here, etiquette intervenes in our story. *We*, we quickly realized, weren't going to be telling them anything. My mother was. It was immediately clear to both of us, especially after the rounds of gender panic we had already been through with her on the subject of what I would wear, that my mother would sooner eat her own liver than try to explain to anyone that her only daughter was a Groom, even if only for the purposes of Filene's. Perhaps if I had been a differently gendered kind of a person, if I had been transsexual and living as a man, or even if I had felt some real attachment to the idea of being a Groom, I would have figured out some quirky, amusing narrative that my mother could be persuaded to use to explain my Groomness. But instead I gladly made the choice to give gendered ground to facilitate ease of gift-giving, especially among those friends of my parents who would be deeply invested in making sure my parents understood they considered my wedding Just Like Any Other Wedding. I had chosen as my mate a woman who is a brilliant cook and confectioner, and I wanted her to have all the top-of-the-line tools she could ever hope for in her kitchen, even if it meant I had to be a Bride to do it.

But back to Margaret, who was still reeling off questions about our lifestyle, which in that moment meant our needs with regard to silver as opposed to stainless and was not a euphemism for anything at all, and who was coming ever closer to the end of her stack of forms and worksheets meant to help us not forget to register for a butter dish or a paring knife. There had been no mention of the bride-or-groomness of anyone. I was not sure if she realized that we were two assigned-female-at-birth people, one of whom was performing that in exactly those ways that suit her and one of whom was edging away from that designation as quick as ze could. I was still not sure how, exactly, I was going to explain this.

"Now then," Margaret said briskly, having checked the final box with a flourish, "let's get you two into the computer." She put her half-glasses back on her nose and squinted at what I would bet good money she referred to as "that infernal machine." She twiddled keys a moment, brought up a fresh screen, and with a satisfied nod turned to Nicole, indicated me with a lift of her chin and asked, "I suppose we're listing this one as the groom?"

Calm as ever, Nicole replied, "No, I'm the groom today. We're taking turns."

"Very sensible," Margaret replied, and asked her to spell our names.

WHITE BUTTON-DOWN SHIRTS

There were years of fights about clothes. Aren't there always? Every butch I know—every single one I have ever met—remembers the day ze looked at the dress of the day or the purple turtleneck with the little pink hearts on it or whatever the offending article of clothing was and said, "Sorry, but no way."

We backed up our No Ways by "losing" the blue culottes and paying it back a dollar a week out of our allowance for being so careless with the one item of good clothes in our summer wardrobes. We wet ourselves at school so we could borrow sweatpants from the drawer of spares for kids who got too covered in piss, paint, or mud to keep those soiled things on; we played in a decidedly unladylike fashion, showing our days-of-the-week panties to all and sundry until Miss Gibson called home so many times that our mothers finally gave in and let us go to school in cords. We stole our brothers' clothes and wore those. We hid plain black T-shirts in our lockers and swapped them out for the atrocity of the day we'd left our houses in. We wore boxer shorts under our schoolgirl kilts. Whether the rebellion was overt or covert, public or private, we said No and we meant it.

I fought with my mother about my clothes for years, an endless number of trips to The Limited, infinite iterations of buying things that I hated, like the infamous jodhpurs of 1988. That was the year that jodhpurs were in fashion for schoolgirls, and every twelve-year-old had a pair. Mine were mauve, and corduroy (no, they really were), and they had four brass buttons up each ankle, and they were perhaps the ugliest, most ill-fitting item of clothes

I had ever, ever seen, but of course my mother had seen some other little girl, lithe as a snake and damn near as sweet, in a similar item. I was already getting so fat that I couldn't wear a lot of what the other girls wore, and here was a pair of pants that looked like what all the cute cool girls were wearing, and in my size, and I can only imagine that my mother thought that these were going to be the magic pants that made me pretty and popular, the way she had always been.

I wore them twice, maybe, and then left them crumpled on the floor of my closet, under my cleats, until they were really thoroughly ruined, for which I took a long scolding that was much less painful than having to put on those pants. After that came years of sweatshirts and sweaters, rugby pullovers and jeans, mostly girls' sizes and colors with maybe the occasional oversized sweatshirt from the men's department, until that magic day when my father, having noticed that other young girls sometimes would do this, offered me some of his old white dress shirts to wear.

My mother immediately began planning ways to girl-ify them with rhinestones, and I'm sure my dad imagined that I would belt them with one of the dozen "cute" belts in my closet, or wear them tied at my waist like a beach-party girl looking to go bad. I put the first one on, feeling the smooth, cool, white cotton on my skin like music, buttoned it up, tucked it in, fastened my cuffs, and smiled at myself in the mirror. *Yeah*, I thought. *Now this is more like it.*

I went downstairs in my blue jeans and Dexter boat shoes and white button-down, my father's blocky monogram still showing at the cuff, feeling good in my body for the first time in recent memory. I bounced down the stairs and walked into the kitchen looking, I'm sure, like a prep-school boy on a Sunday afternoon, despite my head of unfortunate permed-sprayed-and-shellacked hair and a pair of purple glasses so large and hyperfeminine that Sally Jessy Raphael would have bought them right off my face. I walked into the kitchen, they turned and saw me, and their faces fell. They expected me to come downstairs cute in my daddy's clothes, but I came down as myself in my own man's shirt, and the impact of my immense comfort and pleasure, palpable perhaps especially for being so rare, left another crack in their image of the woman I was supposed to be becoming.

I took the shirts back up to my room and hung them carefully in my closet and I wore them all the time; when my mother tried to take me back to The Limited I told her in the flattest possible voice that I wouldn't go, that there was nothing there I wanted to wear, and that anything we bought and spent good money on would sit in my closet and just gather dust, that if she wanted to buy me clothes we could look at the Lands' End catalog together, but that otherwise I would be perfectly happy wearing my father's shirts.

And I did. And I was. Every six months or year he would decommision a bundle of shirts for having frayed collar points or tiny pen marks, and I would adopt them and wear them with pride, like armor, until I started to buy dress shirts of my own, with my own monogram, so I could always have that feeling, so I could always have the option of waking up in the morning to a blazing white dress shirt, stiff with starch, crackling over my heart.

VIRTUAL BUTCH REALITY

In the fall of 1990, when I was a junior in high school, my class-mate Devin introduced me to a wonderful new technology in the form of America Online. With the computers in the school lab and his Hayes 1200 baud modem, I signed on. At five dollars per hour, I tried to be sparing in my usage at first, but I was one of those kids—the kind that always felt more comfortable talking to adults—and the online community at that time was comprised entirely of people adventuresome enough of spirit to understand the allure of AOL and computer-savvy enough to get it to work: I was hooked, instantly.

Not coincidentally, I was also coming out at that time, starting to understand myself as some flavor of queer, and one day, quite by accident, I saw a chat room labeled Gay Chat. This, please understand, was an aberration in a time when public chat rooms could not have the words gay or lesbian, bisexual or transgender in them. People would open them up with some regularity, but when they were noticed by the AOL Powers That Be they would be made into private rooms that couldn't be seen unless a user knew that they were there.

Once you were in the know, you'd sign on and try to go into the private room Lambda Lounge, and if anyone else "in the club" was online, they'd already be in there. Later there were women-only chats, for which one had to be voice-verified as a woman over the phone by allowing the chat mistress, the inimi-table Dorsie Hathaway, to call you collect at home and chat with you for a while to make sure you weren't a het guy named Bob from East Someplace getting his jollies listening in on lesbian life.

All I wanted was access to the women's chats where—I knew from offhanded comments made by older lesbian friends—all the action was. At fifteen years old and almost entirely novice to any possible permutation of the traditional dating-and-mating business of adolescence, action was exactly what I wanted. As a boarding school student in a dormitory, I couldn't accept a collect phone call, and so I had to beg Dorsie to allow me to give her my calling-card number so that we could have this fateful conversation. I assure you that no one has ever pleaded so sincerely to give hir calling-card number away to a stranger ze had met on the Internet. Eventually, Dorsie agreed to call me, and it was all very fine, though it did require me to pace the hallway of my dorm for twenty minutes, keeping my hallmates away from the phone so I could receive this very important call. And so that no one would answer, and speak to her and know (because, of course, such a thing would be discernible by phone) that I was taking a phone call from a Much Older Lesbian.

Eventually you could have a gay chat room, but only one, and then there was a whole gay area, but nothing could be bi or trans, and then slowly over the next four years, the online community of AOL got tolerant and started taking tiny steps toward accepting. There I was, miraculously, sixteen years old with unfettered, un-monitored access to a whole community of older, smarter queers with a lot to say. I asked hundreds of dollars' worth of questions; we talked and talked about everything I could think of and some things which had, frankly, never occurred to me.

They helped me edit my coming-out letter to my family,

which made it very good but also very *long*, and everyone waited with collectively bated breath for the reply and rejoiced when it was good. I felt like part of something exceptional, secret, and all mine, like the mascot of a club of really cool big kids.

The women of those online communities, the chat rooms and the bulletin boards, many of them old-school femmes, must have seen an opportunity to raise my young butch self from scratch into the image of the gentleman butch they would have wanted to meet at sixteen, and they lavished attention and information and praise on me. They taught me, in chat and online, how to give women extravagant compliments that would make them blush without going overboard into ridiculousness, how to ask a girl for a date with charm and style, how to flirt, how to bring a girl a drink or help her on with her coat. The message boards were full of advice on escorting women while shopping, while dancing, to the theater, on what to wear, what flower to buy, and how to present it.

These estimable femmes of all sexes (because, of course, some were transwomen, and some were femme men living their inner-lesbian lives online, and some were as unclassifiable as I felt, back then) were so sweet with me as I stumbled around without a sense of propriety except for what I knew instinctively, and unfolded the secrets of butch and femme for me as though I was a disciple. They took chances and talked with me about sex, explaining how they liked to be touched, and where, teaching me in great detail what magic butches could work with our hands and mouths and cocks.

They told me the inner secrets of their bodies, making my hands sometimes gentle on my lovers and sometimes hard and demanding. Making my mouth an instrument of delight for women in all the years since by teaching me to kiss the mouth of a femme and worry later about where the lipstick was going, by confiding how much they liked to see a butch mouth smeared with their colors. They taught me to bite and then lick away the sting, and a hundred other things, each more intimate than the last. They taught me to come to any bed with a girl in it as though it and she were a privilege.

The trannygirls, especially, schooled me that femme was a gender all its own, that my attraction to them as femmes made me a butch and not in any way a het girl *or* a het guy. They settled any confusion I might later have developed about sexual orientation by showing me the lies of biology and then letting me ask them to dance, letting me give them my jackets when they got cold. All this took place in chat rooms, in virtual space, where everything was safe enough to be played with. Of course, much later, years later, while talking with friends about the good old days, I discovered that many of the transfemmes who soothed and delighted me with their patient and gentle willingness to play were just as grateful to my nascent butch self for giving *them* the same chance to expand into femininity under my wholly uncritical gaze, and for making them feel beautiful and desired, like forties silver-screen queens, like Bond Girls.

Strangely, other butches were largely silent or absent on the boards in those days, maybe for class reasons, maybe because of the myth of the "real" butch who is monosyllabic and reserved, but there were a few, especially in the later years when the Women of Leather boards were available to us, and they taught me, too. Taught me to keep my confidences and to count my blessings, and, maybe above all the other lessons, that my survival depended on being able to turn to the brotherhood in times of trouble.

That meant being big enough to admit when I was in over my head, it meant being smart enough to recognize when that was, and it meant being respectful enough to be a part of that brotherhood, rather than at cross-purposes with it. I met my first butches who loved butches, the first but certainly not last of that quiet breed, and I felt delighted and amazed to know that I wasn't the only queer sort of queer who looked at the old bull on the street, or the woman truck driver at the post office, and melted down my legs and into my boots with the thought of wrapping my arms around the trunk of hir.

The magic of this community, then, these butches and these femmes, was that I spent the first few of my formative butch years blissfully free of anyone's ideas about butch life except that of my mentors, who did not disagree with one another but rather spread out their experiences before me like the best goods at a bazaar and watched to see what I picked up first, and then told me the history and properties, pleasures and dangers of what I'd touched.

I learned all of this through text on a screen. I sat in the computer lab of my high school, shielding the green-on-black CRT with my body leaning in close, drinking in every scrap of knowledge offered and saving the chat logs for later so that I could read them again. I was looking for clues and patterns, trying to read between the lines of the life I intended to lead. People I had never met in person—some of whom I never would meet—took me at my word and spent their money and their time taking care of me, in the days when everything online happened at the speed of trees and cost five bucks an hour to do it. Like priests with no idea who sat on the other side of the confessional box, they listened and advised me. I was so grateful.

I may have been the first one ever, the blessed little child or fool who wandered in at the exact right moment—I don't know. What I do know is that if I had turned up, at sixteen, at a dyke bar, I would have been ejected, and if I had been miraculously and illegally admitted by some softhearted bouncer, I would have been roundly laughed at for my clothes and my hair and probably sent away by mob rule. But online, I was safe from all of this. No one could see my clothes or my unfortunate hair; they could only know me through my words, and through the fire of my butch heart, and that's what they respected as they so sweetly gave me the keys to a kingdom.

THE HONORABLE BUTCH OFFICE OF MOVING

I still know her, and I'll always remember her—Sally Brown, the diva bartender of our local Homo Hotspot, a whole generation older than me and the first old-school femme woman I ever met in person, wearing red, wet lipstick and rose water, wearing Lycra and boots.

It's the first day we've met. Someone I know a little bit introduces us at the bar, and I am just as delighted and gobsmacked by the power of her femme energy as I ever am again with any femme. I order a soda, I stumble a little on my words, sonicetomeetyou, and I flee out of range of her gaze, and her perfume.

When I go back for a refill, I set my glass on the counter and she sees me, comes right over, and before I can ask anything, she reaches out her hand and puts it on my forearm, sliding the tips of her fingers along the sensitive skin right there, skin so sensitive they craft transmen's new dicks from it. I can smell her perfume again, and it's like the finger of scent you see in Wile E. Coyote cartoons when the soup or pie beckons him entirely against his will, following him out the window and curling its ethereal talon into his nostrils and dragging him back to the dangerous place by the sensitive parts. She looks at me through her eyelashes, through lidded eyes, and spreads her hand out on my forearm and says, "So, handsome. What are you doing with these muscles on Saturday?"

I take a deep breath and, with reasonable aplomb given the fact that all the blood has fled my brain for parts south, say something to the effect of "Nothing special. What did you have in mind?" At which point she leans in closer, close enough so that one of her breasts is almost sitting in the palm of my open hand and says, with a purr in her voice:

"Want to help me move?" Well? I've just said I'm not doing anything on Saturday. I agree. She gives me her number on a slip of paper and puts it on the bar between us, and refills my soda, and I wander away, a little stunned, trying to figure out whether this is perhaps a euphemism. But I resolve to turn up on Saturday, and in fact I do, and there assembled at Sally's house is a collection of people who are supposed to help with the moving, or some such thing, and so I figure this will be a couple hours of hauling and then I'll go have my day. However hornswoggled I felt for the way in which I ended up agreeing to this, I can see that Sally Brown is a femme of the old school, gorgeous and tough as hell, and as soon as I see her on her front steps that morning, holding a cigarette between red fingernails and wearing the damn cutest bandanna on her head I've ever seen, my good gentleman butch upbringing fills me afresh with the desire to be helpful to her. I roll up my sleeves and get to work.

Of course, there are developments. Several of the assembled are artists, and cannot risk damage to their hands from touching anything heavy or sharp. These women move the couch cushions, the bed linens, and the trash bags into which Sally Brown has emptied her dresser drawers. Then they sit in the sun at the new place and chat about the evils of creeping commercialism. Also present are a gaggle of femme acquaintances of Sally Brown's, who are there to help her unpack and set up in the new place. They hold doors open for me, help me get unsnagged when my belt loops take a liking to protruding items, and make lemonade.

This is not to suggest that any of them couldn't have moved almost anything I could have, but ... they didn't. This leaves me and a fiftyish butch named Mary Lee to do the rest of the heavy lifting.

Eight hours later I struggle sweatily into the new place with the last overstuffed armchair, wearing it on my head like a Hat Sister gone horribly wrong, and place it in the new apartment at the direction of Sally Brown in the precise spot she indicates, and stand up, and use the hem of my T-shirt to wipe my face, and Sally Brown reaches up and brushes a lock of hair out of my face, and smiles at me and says, "Thanks, Bear," so sweetly, fixing my eyes with her fern-colored ones, saying something more than that to me in the timeless manner of femmes that I was just then beginning to understand, speaking softly in the small space between us.

Now, in retrospect, I understand that she was thanking me not only for having spent my day schlepping for a relative stranger, she was thanking me for being a butch, for turning up at her bar and being the kind of young but not unschooled kid whom she could recognize at a glance and take into her confidence without fear.

Since that day I have moved dozens of girls into more dozens of apartments because I can, and because they could use the help, and because I like to be helpful more than I like to be almost anything else. But mostly because at the end of the day they always preen my sweaty hair a little bit and say a quiet thank you just to me.

PASSING IT ALONG

Fifteen years ago, when I came out (which makes me feel like the ancient of days, when in fact I just came out a bit ahead of schedule), I had role models, older butches and femmes, who were there to help me navigate the rocky shoals of queer dating. I am not sure I realized how much I learned from them, and how important the lessons were, until just this afternoon, which I spent in a dark bar with a recently out butch just a half-dozen years younger than me. It isn't the elapsed time since birth, sometimes, but the elapsed-time-since-rebirth, since one's heart and, not incidentally, loins make themselves known.

Ze'd had a fairly common first experience of queer dating for someone in a smallish town, known as "you'll be my girlfriend because you're the only other dyke I know," spending two years with a perfectly nice girl in a relationship that didn't really do it for either of them. Recently, and with a refreshing lack of animosity, they had broken up. Bringing us to the current moment. This little dykelet had met a femme the previous night and had no idea what to do. None. The femme was clearly full of signals and cues, expectations and ideas, and the young butch with whom I sat barely recognized any of them and certainly had no idea what to do about them.

Ze had never dated a femme before and was feeling somewhere between "in over hir head" and "out of hir league," except that the femme had made it more than clear that she expected to hear from my new friend sometime in the near future. The urgency of the matter, and a total lack of anywhere to turn for advice, had led hir to the cool cave of this bar in the afternoon, where Sally Brown (ten years after the first story in which she appears) and I tried to start at the beginning and give hir enough information and encouragement to make some difference.

It was a strangely intimate encounter, considering that we'd never met before. I was acutely aware of it as we sat and talked, and we ate the fries I'd ordered and offered to share, and shared a cigarette, passing it casually back and forth and talking about girls. At first it felt strange, as though we'd skipped quite a few steps and gone directly to advanced friendship, to this serious-hearted sharing of confidences about love and relationships, to this place where I was speaking about my butch heart.

After a while, though, it started to feel different; it seemed like just another iteration of a conversation that has been going on for G-d alone knows how many years, between how many elder butches and younger ones, the tribal passing of information that has happened since butches stood upright and took up spears. As though it was so easy to sit and talk that way because the conversation already knew its own shape, and all we needed to do was be there and let it spin itself out between us. Which I hope is true.

The thing that struck and saddened me most, though, was that in order to get this information, ze had to go to a bar and hope for the kindness of a total stranger. What would have happened if I hadn't turned up, if Sally hadn't been working, if no one with the old way of mentoring that she and I share had been present to call those words out of our tribal history for this youngster? Where would ze have turned?

We have started, as evolving cultures do, to record our traditions in writing and art, but that would have been no good at all in this case. How do we make sure, as a tribe, that our new members are getting a chance to ask questions and not just coming to the bars thinking they're supposed to know it all already?

I had my lessons from an estimable elder butch, our silver-haired, no-nonsense Uncle Pam. I spent more hours than I could possibly count sitting on the porch of her house, eating whatever her partner Deb had cooked and listening to her talk about the old days, about what it meant to be a butch. When I had questions or problems or needed advice on the ways of femmes especially, I would seek out Uncle, who gave me a million pieces of information and, maybe more importantly, taught me by example how to give a proud, arrogant youngster information ze desperately needs without being condescending about it.

I am terrified to think about even trying to fill her shoes and also exhilarated that someone, even this one butch in a bar on a Sunday afternoon, thinks I might be able to. I know that Uncle thinks so, too. On my thirtieth birthday she gave me one of her ties, and if that's not the butch seal of approval, then I can't imagine what it might be.

Maybe it's a moot point, these days. Maybe *Queer Eye for the Straight Guy* and *The L Word*, Gay-Straight Alliances in high schools and Queer Centers in colleges have rendered the need for community-mentoring obsolete. But I don't think so. I don't think that the hair-product lessons one can learn from television shows nor the peer support one can have in GLBT school groups is the same as being able to sit down with someone who has been there, and say: What do I do? What should I expect? Why does this hurt so much? How can I always feel this good?

I want them to be able to ask, and I want us—if I can imagine myself elder enough to give advice—to make space for the asking to happen. I'd like to think that other queers out there are keeping track of the fact that the younger generation needs mentors and role models, if we expect them to feel powerful, supported, loved, and safe the way I did. I know so many younger butches and boys who have so many questions, who need to know so many things.

What is keeping us from making ourselves resources for this next generation? As butches especially, we keep our fire inside— our proudest moments and our shameful ones, our mistakes and our triumphs—and sometimes it burns us instead of fueling us, sometimes we see our mistakes and our shames far too clearly, we imagine ourselves unfit or unworthy to try to teach anyone else anything about anything at all.

It's no wonder, as much as heteronormative society calls us unfit and unworthy, as much as we struggle to be accepted and loved as the paradoxical, complicated, mythical creatures we are. Maybe we imagine in our secret hearts that if we deny young butches counsel, if it is too hard for them to sort everything out, that they will turn back to a less dangerous path and be safer than we could ever make them. It does seem some days like giving someone detailed and careful instructions for putting one's hand in the snowblower.

I am trying to add new lessons to the chorus of butch that I sing out to the next generation, trying to re-ingrain the sacred butch duty of mentoring the next generation. Maybe it isn't my place, but I'm trying to shout my conviction that, as a butch, just surviving the gender violence and constriction of this world to be old enough to speak truth to the next wave qualifies us to give advice, teach the values of butch, its form and mode, its sweet call-and-response; that just being alive and sober to tell it is enough credentials for anyone.

BOXER BRIEFS

The same year I cut my hair short, I started wearing men's underwear. Someone gave me a pair of soft, gray cotton jersey boxer shorts, and I fell in love with them. They were far more comfortable than my Jockey For Her briefs, no unfinished seams chafing the tender spot where my leg meets my body, that soft place that should never be subjected to elastic. And I felt more confident in them, more attractive in them, like taking off some of my clothes in front of an object of desire would be a far better proposition if taking off my pants didn't result in me trying to make hir melt in my arms while clad in panties. I understand that this works out just fine for some people, but not for me. A T-shirt and boxer shorts, or even just the shorts, let me imagine myself taller, more handsome, stronger, sexier. I felt good in the space I was taking up, all of a sudden; I felt more confident in my clothes and out of them. Slowly, I started throwing out my Jockeys For Her and buying more boxer shorts.

I hadn't really considered how this might play at home, however. I was still a college student, and brought my laundry home at breaks, as college students will. When my mother first saw my boxer shorts (the dryer finished, and I was too slow to empty it) she waved them at me questioningly, both—I think—hoping and fearing that their appearance in my laundry was a direct result of a boy in my bed. I explained that they were mine, that I had switched, and managed to make a case for them being cute, remembering in the dimness of my brain a fad from my days at camp in which girls wore men's boxers with festive things printed on them as shorts. I told her I thought they were comfy and fun.

Fun, if I recall correctly, was the exact word I used. She bought it. We tacitly hid them from my father who, I suspected, was not going to be as willing to get on board with his only daughter—the apple of his eye—wearing men's underwear on a regular basis.

Shortly after this, boxer briefs were introduced to the underpants-wearing public, and I was instantly a convert. I bought several pairs and was always on the lookout for more, as very few manufacturers made them at that time. They were even better than boxer shorts, just as comfortable but with a much lower tendency to climb up my ass as I walked. Besides which, they fit my thighs rather than fluttering about as the boxer style sometimes did. I did not want a flutter in my manly underwear.

Chief among the innovators was Calvin Klein, and so during a family trip to the outlet malls in Kittery, Maine, Mom and I went over to CK to see whether we could pick me up a few more pair. We did. These had a new innovation: two buttons on the fly. I was in underwear heaven. I could just imagine myself in my black boxer briefs with the buttoned fly, so soft and sexy, taking off my pants in front of a cute girl and feeling not an ounce of discomfort. I put the bag with the four new pair in the trunk and got back in the car with my folks and brother, and we headed up the road to The Weathervane, a sprawling seafood emporium right there on US 1 in Maine, for a big family lunch.

Until my father looked in the trunk.

Suddenly he was brandishing my underwear literally over his head, asking my mother whether that was what she had bought for me at Calvin Klein. When she allowed that it was, he turned red in the face and screamed at the top of his lungs, demanding to know why she had done it, and why I was wearing them, and what

the hell was going on. He went absolutely ballistic, full-tilt boo-
gie on a sunny afternoon in the parking lot of The Weathervane,
in view of all and sundry, and certainly within hearing of any
interested party. Whenever anyone says gender panic these days
in the panels I go to or the books I read, this is always the image
that flashes across my brainpan: someone's father in a parking lot
somewhere having the screaming fantods over some distinctly
other-gendered underthings.

My father saw me more clearly in that moment than nearly
everyone else, even through his rage. He must have known that
the short hair and then the men's underwear in the space of six
months was not a positive sign that I was well on the way to becoming the daughter he had imagined: the smart-and-tough-but-
also-feminine-and-pretty girl he started thinking about when I
appeared on the scene in the autumn of 1974. Several pieces came
into focus for him for the first time. He looked at me with a mix-
ture of wonder and horror that I don't think I've seen since, for a
long moment, before continuing to rant and rave about what the
hell and I'm not paying for this and how dare you, and so on. He
stormed back toward the restaurant, I announced that I would be
walking back to Connecticut, he told me that I oughtn't bother
going back to Connecticut as I wouldn't be allowed in the house
when I got there—we were *great* arguers—until my mother came
back outside and made us shut up and come inside and sit down
and eat lunch. My father and I glowered at each other across the
table.

We didn't mention the incident again. I started piling my
men's underwear on the top of my folded laundry when I came
home at school breaks, and I kept wearing them, feeling quietly,

unaccountably sexy in them. I kept my mouth shut when, a year later, Dad started wearing the same style and brand of boxer briefs as I did, and my mother had to take a laundry marker to his so we could tell them apart in the folding piles on the family room floor.

WHERE BUTCH RESIDES

Sometimes I think it's in my hands. They're big, you know, big boy paws, big enough to hold two glasses in each when I'm carrying them back to the table. Sometimes sort of grubby, sometimes clean and well clipped, sweaty in her cool and dry ones when we walk, arms swinging slightly down the street. They are hands that capably twist jars open, twist wire around contact points, twist nails out of wood, but also hold her so gently, soft enough to cradle a newborn between them safely against my heart, pick a dock splinter out of a smooth thigh; steady enough to make pleasure between, to hold hopes between. Sometimes when I sit and think about where it is that my butch self begins, I feel the power and gentleness in my hands, warm and heavy where they rest on my thighs, and it seems like that's where it must be.

Other days, I think it's in my shoulders. They're big, too, not that you have to be big to be butch, but I sometimes think it helps; large of stature or of persona anyway. They're lean-on shoulders, cry-on shoulders, shoulders upon which I can comfortably bear a lot of weight; I put them down against hard times and I push, using whatever power I can find or borrow or draw up from my web of friends, and things move, however slowly, but they move. I square my shoulders when it looks like it might get tough. I puff up like any wild animal when it gets cornered; I try to look large enough to be a threat. I feel my jacket hang down just so, my shirts stretch slightly across the expanse of my back, and I feel the power of butch rush across my shoulders and down my back so it looks in my mind like in the outdoor shower when I stand there in just trunks, letting the warm water pour down.

Maybe in my hips, somewhere around my thighs, not my cock or my cunt per se, but a near neighbor, a sexual organ all its own, something desirous and desired. My butchness engorges at the approach of an object of my desire, it leads the way and I follow, bringing along my butch behaviors all fed with the strength of that blood, those muscles, that possibility of my womb. I lead with my hips, my butch does the walking and I'm along for the ride. I reach out with my helping or my gallantry or my sexuality or my gentleness, and it throbs with begging to be touched, acknowledged, wanted. Wanted for being exactly what it is, at its most when someone welcomes it into hirself, tenderly or roughly, or when it is able to take someone in, make hir feel desired or soothed in some way. It changes its parts like an earthworm in response to its partner and seems always to have the right thing.

Many days it seems, though, to live in my chest, in a place in my ribcage very close to my heart. I feel it beating there, sometimes swelling so large it makes my chest hurt in a beautiful, perfect way unlike anything else, like getting a little too much air after a day playing in the snow or the sea; I get a really big lungful and it feels so full, so sweet, so absolutely perfect that I wish it could always feel just like that. It blazes in my chest so bright I'm surprised people can't see it, warm and glowing, not surprised that it attracts predators; surprised every time when I try to describe it—though I have so many words, and can pull fire out of the air with them—and I can't get a tenth of the way there. It lives in my chest and glows and lights my way, and beats and keeps me warm. It makes me find new ways every day to show love and care, and rises to meet each challenge, and rises to every occasion as best it can; it rises and I follow it, beyond the reach of where my brain can go, or my hands or shoulders or sex, it rises up to where truth lives in our lives, and that means I get to go there too.

THAT MOMENT

I was just about to turn six, and I had planned it. I knew exactly what I was going to do, and how I was going to defend myself if I was caught. It is the first time in my life I remember planning an alibi for a gender crime, but not the last time, not by a long shot.

The following things were involved: one cup of juice, one hot August day, one swing. One T-shirt.

All summer long Brent, who lived a few houses down and was my frequent playmate when his mother wasn't scolding me for being unladylike, had been swinging on my swing set with me. I had a very, *very* cool swing set: a dark green wood, Child-Life brand, top-of-the line swing set with two regular swings, a bouncy swing, two chains that would attach a trapeze or a pair of rings, a teeter-totter, a slide, a climbing cargo net, a small jungle gym with premade inserts for fort-making, and monkeybars.

It had been the combined gift of both sets of grandparents, a far nicer swing set than anyone of our means or our neighbors could afford, and I loved it, spending all day on it with my play-mates. Including Brent who, this particular summer, had discovered, probably by virtue of his older brother, the habit of taking his shirt off on hot summer days. There he would be, swinging happily away next to me, wearing nothing but a pair of filthy shorts (we were always under the deck, which stood about a foot off the ground, though I could not tell you what it was we found so exciting under there) and a great big, flying-through-the-air grin. I was similarly attired, except for a dirty T-shirt, which I was told I had to keep on the few times I tried to remove it earlier in the summer, at the beginning of Brent's shirtless phase.

I wanted to run around in just shorts, pee wherever I wanted, and hose myself clean-ish after coming out from under the deck. I gave up on peeing wherever I wanted after a few unfortunate incidents in the reedy vacant lot behind my house, and hosing myself off was never really that exciting, especially because it turned out that not being able to do it meant holding the hose for Brent, which meant shooting water up his nose, or on his shorts, et cetera, and so on. But the just-shorts thing. That I really wanted.

So I waited for a hot day. I waited for a day that my mother left my lunch on the table and went back upstairs to take care of my just-toddling brother. I took my lunch outside to eat on the deck, and I ate the sandwich and the carrot sticks, then took one sip of juice, and poured the rest of it right down my shirt and a little bit onto my shorts, as well, which I had not counted on. I removed my shirt. Then I went over to the hose, turned it on, washed the sticky juice off my tiny torso, and headed for the swings.

It was wonderful. It was just as good as I imagined it being, shirtless in the sun on a hot day with the breeze from swinging made cool by the water drying on my skin. Suddenly my throat was full of envy and anger at Brent, blithely enjoying this great pleasure all summer long by birthright, and if he had been there I don't know what I would have said or done. As it was, I stayed on the swing until I had swung myself dry, then jumped off and did it all again, rolling around in the grass like a dog first to see what that felt like. The grass was tickly and soft on my belly, cool on my back. I could feel an ant crawling up onto me. I got back on the swing set and stayed there, singing to myself and swinging until my mother came outside and saw me.

When she started scolding, I explained that it had *just hap-pened*, that I had spilled (see?) and then washed off my sticky dirty self without making a mess inside (see?) but I was in the middle of making up a new song so I just jumped back on the swing for a *second*, Mom, (see?) and I was just about to come in, any second.

I don't remember if I got in trouble or not. Probably not. It seems unlike my sensible mother to be too upset about such a thing, and I had very carefully and specifically spilled apple juice, and not grape, so I hadn't ruined my shirt with my carelessness. But I remember the risk seeming enormous, and I remember the immense pleasure of standing shirtless and barefooted in the summer sun like it was a triumph, like it was proof of something.

It still feels that way. When I can be shirtless and barefoot in shorts or blue jeans on a sunny day, padding around in some private enclave or lazing in a pool or a river with my wife and friends, I always wet my head and chest so I can feel like that again, like coming home in my body for the first time, like that moment, the first utterly right moment. So far, I haven't been able to get a swing set into the equation. But I'm working on it.

WHAT MY DADDY TAUGHT ME

I'm sitting with this great Minnesota girl I know now, and we're talking about the home improvements I'm doing—how I'm learning to spackle and paint, level and plumb—and she tells me that she put in a whole new kitchen at her old place, tells me that she once changed the engine mount in a Ford truck, that she can re-wire near about anything that has a wire to its name, and she says, "My daddy taught me how." She's proud and she should be. She clearly loves him and everything he taught her to do, the words coming out bright and crisp as I imagine a Minnesota spring sky must be, the kind that would have sheltered her as she got dirty with her dad under the truck on a May afternoon.

My dad? He taught me to pay attention, and to take care of the people I love. Also that I should do what I was good at, and ask for help with things I didn't know about.

For cars, he taught me that 1-800-AAA-HELP is the emergency roadside number for Triple A, and gave me a membership when I got my first car. On plumbing, he taught me to turn the faucet off all the way and that if I ever needed a plumber I should ask my friends rather than calling out of the phone book and tip the guy so he'd come back the next time if I needed him.

But his lessons of community were gentlemen's lessons, butch lessons, given over the years as much by action as in instruction, and I absorbed them all. I learned to not only listen to what people said but to watch what they did, and not only that but to re-member, and to synthesize that information so that in the future I might be able to anticipate some need in someone I loved and help them before they even asked. To watch carefully and see fully all of those things that are important to my friends and family, and to keep that aggregate of information at the forefront of my consciousness, to see the entire world through a filter of what the people I know and love might want or need, heedless of current thinking about codependency or self-actualization or whatever other bullshit disguised as modern medicine or self-help made it into the mainstream consciousness. That no matter how taxing it might be in the short term, the benefits in my life would be priceless, that I too could end up like my grandparents, whose friends still living danced at my wedding because we had known each other my whole life and they were as much my family as my blood relatives. That I could have the same friends for fifty years. That's what my daddy taught me.

A real friend, he'd say, is the one who, when you say you need for them to kill someone for you, asks only, "And where did you want me to dump the body?" I understood that it was hyperbole, but I saw him do barely less more than once, to exhaust himself in research and effort to help *his* people. Which is how he divided the whole world: his people and everyone else. He'd be perfectly willing to lend a hand to everyone else if he could, if they asked, but he would have lain down in traffic for one of his people if they needed him to and never counted the cost.

He never created a sense of obligation, but just did the thing that needed to be done and then went on to the next thing, in the midst of providing for his family and being a pillar of our temple and a variety of other things we never knew about because he never spoke about them, he just did them. He might yell and carry on, he might curse your stupidity for getting into a jam, but he'd always help. That's what my daddy taught me.

So now I go on, doing exactly as I learned from him to do, surprising my loved ones with the magnitude of my attention, both the depth and the breadth of it upon which they remark as though it were something extraordinary but which seems perfectly natural to me. Watching them be shocked that I remember I saw them once get a flat and not know how to change it in the middle of the night and it was cold, so I sneak a can of Fix-a-Flat and an encouraging little note and my phone number into the compartment where the tire-changing items live, and they call me out of the blue from some roadside a year later laughing and crying at the same time to say help and thanks and I love you, which is exactly what I said to my father all the time, feeling so well taken care of, and so beloved.

It is exactly how I want my friends and family to feel because I love them so. I buy a little present and put it in my bag and then put it in the right pocket of the right pair of pants days in advance in anticipation of that stressful moment when she's going to need a little cheering up, so I can reach into my jeans and present her with a little something in that difficult moment, just because I love her, not just that moment but also three days ago at the store. I'm on my feet to make tapioca as soon as I hear another friend clear his throat over the phone, because last December he had a horrible, virulent strep and it sounded just like that three days in advance, and I'm at his house with pudding and soup noodles and packing him off to the doctor while he's still in denial because I don't want it to get worse. I say, "That's just what it sounded like last year," and he makes a face at me and says, "How the hell do you remember that?" and I think: I remember because I love you, and because you are my family and without you my life wouldn't even be worth living, and because I want you to be well and happy all the time, and because that's what my daddy taught me.

FOIE D'BUTCH

The human liver is the largest and one of the most important internal organs of the body, weighing in at just a bit over three pounds. It is responsible for guarding against harmful agents as they pass through by altering them, filtering them out, or destroying them. It has a dual blood supply, and it uses and filters and alters and heals every bit of blood that passes through it until it fails or the person dies. It balances blood sugar and proteins, hormones and adrenaline. It produces the substances that allow blood clotting for the healing of wounds, and can regenerate itself with stunning ability. Fast enough that when doctors at Cedars-Sinai hospital created a bioengineered liver and tested it as a stopgap solution for people in end-stage liver failure—a stage in which ninety percent of patients die waiting for a transplant and for which the bioengineered liver was supposed to help by giving them a few more precious days until a match might be found—four of them never needed transplants, because the bioengineered liver had kept going long enough for their own livers to recover and regenerate.

The French, it is said, possess an organ that no other people of the world have: the *foie d'amour* (fwah d'ah-more), literally, the liver of love. It is this organ, according to myth and legend, which allows the French to digest an array of difficulties related to the emotion of love, from bliss to betrayal, and live with them or excrete them as the case demands. When we hear stories of the classic French tolerance for the vagaries and affairs of the heart like the famous one of Prime Minister François Mitterand's wife and mistress standing next to one another at his funeral, we are hearing the stories of the *foie d'amour* at work.

When I talk with elder butches about their lives, when I think about the trajectory of my own and the obstacles I have met along the way, I wonder whether there may in fact be a *foie d'butch*. A separate organ, born or grown, that takes in the damaging and difficult parts of butch life—the otherness and the sorrow, the rejections and the violence, and the nourishing parts of it too, the warmth of the tribe and the balls-deep sense of honor and pride—and then processes and balances and filters them until we are healthy enough to go on. I wonder about what special compound it might produce to heal the wounds of a butch heart, a butch soul: those stark moments in which we know with a certitude that chills the bone that the obstacle we face is not what we do or know but who we are, something we could only change if we were willing to lose our identities to do it. I wonder if it is the *foie d'butch* that is failing when butches of whatever age reach a point at which the difficulties seem too great and the rewards too few, when they become bitter or angry, or withdraw in defeat.

It seems a lovely metaphor, and it just keeps going: of course, it would be in the *foie d'butch* that confidence and strength stored in the body from good and safe moments could be triggered to produce the extra energy needed in times of stress, just as the liver converts stored glycogen to glucose under the same anatomic circumstances. In the *foie d'butch*, as in the liver, the worst diseases are caused by obstructions, by hardening or stubbornness or paralyzation or blockage caused by acute overload, any of which causes the caustic chemicals of the liver, so helpful when contained and doing their jobs, to spill into the rest of the body and begin to consume it. Having to process too many harmful compounds—loss, longing, fear, anger—for too long would eventually cause the *foie d'butch* to falter unless it is given either help or rest.

Because it does seem, many days, as though there must be something. Some reason, some additional aid, some unknown or unseen process that keeps butches doggedly following their hearts, and their hearts' desires, long after similar opposition or resistance would stop many people. And the ideal of butch, however much we may or may not be able to live up to it, is that a butch is both gentle and tough, decisive and ethical, strong and kind, hard-working and playful. Not to mention the neat trick of balancing somehow for millennia in a no-man's-land between man and woman, which I would love to refer to with a less sexist term like DMZ, but it sure as hell ain't that: the forces of gender come for butches every day, and they must be ready to fight or flee.

On the edges of my thinking and writing about butch I am always grasping for what it is, *exactly*, that makes all this possible. I attribute it to the forging process of butch coming-of-age, to the knowledge that comes with outsider experience, to the unique combination that exists in many butches of being socialized as women, but eventually prized for their masculinity, and the winnowing of gender behaviors that this creates. And I struggle to explain why sometimes someone looks butch (adj.), or acts butch (adv.), and then sometimes, someone is a butch (n.).

I have always thought of this, and spoken of it, as the butch heart, continuing to romanticize that workhorse muscle as the writing of the modern era of the English language has taught me. Not at all surprisingly, some languages are way ahead of us. In Malay, the word for liver is *hati*, and it is viewed as the source of all emotion, even though it is understood as the metaphoric equivalent to the Western notion of "heart." One may be referred to as having a *susah hati*, or literally a "difficult liver," being worried, or as being *baik hati*, good-hearted. A fond endearment for someone much beloved is *buah hati*, or "fruit of my liver."

Maybe the *foie d'butch*, the butch *hati*—heavy, hardworking, delicate, constantly adjusting, constantly soothing the blood and healing the wounds and making the cruelest betrayals somehow possible to live with—is what I have been admiring in butches all these years. Maybe, instead of resting my open hand so gently on the chests of butches as a way to encourage or soothe them, I should be patting bellies, instead. It doesn't quite sound right to say that someone has a great liver. But saying, "That one has a true *foie d'butch*" doesn't sound bad. Not bad at all.

WHEN IT'S GOOD

When it's good, it's perfect.

When it's good, I feel like a knight, everything shining, pennant fluttering, victorious in an honorable cause, wearing my beloved's favor against my heart. Like all the motions of time and space are in my skin with me, enriching my blood and enlivening my nerve endings one by one, like the runway lights along my spine have blinked on. Like I could leap tall buildings in a single bound. When it's good I am with my tribe, casually having coffee and ice cream on the city hall steps in my small New England city, sitting all afternoon and collecting whoever comes along, the sun on our shoulders and our jokes familiar in both senses of the word, like we have the right to that space, and to each other's company, and to our joy. I am walking down the street with my beloved wife, both of us dressed up and coordinated with each other, in step, her hand tucked through the crook of my arm; my eyes are up and my chest is out, there's a spring in my step and I am glad-hearted. I am taking a young butch shopping for hir first dress shirt and tie, watching the helpless delight on hir face as ze catches hir reflection in the mirror for the first time in the crisp shirt, tie looped around hir neck; I stand behind hir and encircle hir with my arms, let hir lean back against the breadth of my chest and carefully watch my movements in the mirror while I knot hir tie. I am riding in the car, in the dark, with a butch I love, speaking our fears and hopes into the quiet that deepens between us, dense with secrets, and somehow in the telling we can both feel heard, and seen, and bound together. I am standing, literally, between someone and trouble—maybe a loved one, maybe just someone who sees me clearly and has asked my help in a difficult moment—standing there planted in my boots, praying that I can just use my size and calm forcefulness to solve the problem, but ready to do what needs to be done and so relieved to be there to do it. I am lifting another small child onto my shoulders for another ride, or spinning hir around until we're both dizzy, or holding hir sweet, slack body against my chest while hir adult or adults watch with fondness and not a bit of concern. I am at the front of a classroom full of undergraduates, inert in their ignorance about gender, explaining and answering and joking while I stand there in my shirt and tie and blue jeans, letting them like me, helping them to understand, leaving them thinking about masculinity as a process and not a product; at the end of the hour I haven't even gotten through all the questions and that's all the time we have for today, the professor says, and they applaud me for a long time, come up in ones and twos after the class ends to tell me how brave they think I am. I am toting the last of the hundred-odd boxes up to the third floor, passing my dearest friends on the way up and down; back at the bottom I take the other end of a dresser and go backward up the stairs with it, slowly but without any fear, having been guided backward up ten years worth of stairs by the same friend, so glad to be helping and also so glad to feel so safe in the competent care of this member of my tribe. I am sitting sneakers to sneakers with a teenaged boy on the precipice of sex, taking advantage of my coyote gender to talk about not just the dangers of sex but also its pleasures, to talk about who has the right to want what, to tell him that her "no" is inviolable but that his "no" counts too, to say that pleasure held carefully between people who are deeply invested in one another is a great gift; I tell him that when he finds someone he wants to please as much as he wants to feel good himself he's on the right track. I am alone in the kitchen in my house, barefooted in just a pair of old shorts, drinking juice straight out of the carton, feeling the play of my back muscles and suddenly, unaccountably feeling so powerful in my body. I am asking a beautiful girl to dance with me, and there is that perfect moment at which she forgets who else is around and whether anyone is watching and gives her weight into my arms, just slightly, just enough to let me know that she is with me for this moment, that we're together in this. I am at the hospital in the middle of the night, sitting next to someone who has had a fall or a finally-too-worrisome cough and called me for help, holding hir hand and stroking hir head and quietly telling funny stories. I am sitting in a strip club and one of the dancers recognizes me as a butch and her smile changes from mechanical to genuine. I am bringing the car around in bad weather. I am bringing the scary, fuzzy spider outside under a glass. I am trying to figure out what you need. I am doing the best I can. I am hoping I am good enough. I am holding you close, as close as I can, hand cradling your head and breath on your hair, my whole body curved around yours, sheltering you as best I can, trying to remember that I cannot keep you safe, but I can keep you loved.

When it's good, it's perfect. When it's good, I remember why I bother trying. When it's good, I feel like I can get home from here.

STICKS AND STONES WILL BREAK MY BONES, BUT WORDS WILL KILL ME

"What the fuck are you supposed to be? Yeah, bitch, I'm talking to you. Don't pretend you don't fucking hear me, dyke. What the fuck is that, a bitch in a tie? You trying to be a man or something? I'll fucking show you what a real man looks like. You ain't got what I got, do you, cunt, do you, huh? Naw, that's what you got, a cunt, a sweet little pink pussy between your legs, not a dick like I got. You wish you had a dick, bitch. Is that it, you fucking freak? I could put a dick between your legs. You wanna be my bitch? You want me to show you what a real man looks like? I could make you real pretty on your knees. Turn around. Turn around, I'm talking to you, butch. Turn around."

"I went out and paid good money and bought you these nice clothes so that you wouldn't be running around look-ing like a farmhand all the time, and I expect you to put them on, young lady, if you want to leave this house with your mother and me. How do you think we feel, being known as the people who have one daughter and one 'it,' hmm? It isn't nice, I can tell you that for sure. Now, here are your new clothes, and your mother is taking all of those others away, and you will stay in this room until you can put on real clothes like a normal human being, and I don't think that's too much to ask."

"I'm so sorry, er, ma'am, but I don't really think we have anything for you here. Perhaps you'd be more comfortable shopping at a store that has a ladies' department. Nothing personal, ma'am, we just don't have any experience dressing ladies. So. Thank you very much for stopping by, and I'll take that suit, thanks, yes, and you have a nice day now. I'm sure you and your, er, companion there will be able to find a different establishment that has something suitable for you."

"If I wanted to be with a man, I would have gone ahead and dated one. I don't know where you're getting all of this male energy there, with your little tie and your sock or whatever that is that you have between your legs, but I became a lesbian so that I could be with a woman, not some kind of a fake man in a cheap suit. You're setting the feminist movement back fifty years in your little getup. I don't understand why you can't be a real woman and be normal, like everyone else. You're just aping patriarchal models, trying to blend in to the phallocracy, trying to take away my sacred womon-loving womon power by invisibilizing me as a lesbian, and you're oppressing women in general and lesbians in particular and me most especially by coming around looking and acting that way. I am not going anywhere with you!"

"I just don't get you, man. Why the hell would you want to get down with a sweaty, hairy butch when you've got hot girls hanging all over you? Are you some kind of fag or something? You better not be thinking shit like that about me. Butches are for femmes, man, and femmes are for butches. Look at all those girls, looking at us, they all think you're hot, why don't you take one of them for a spin, eh? Come on, my femme's best friend is here. I'll introduce you, she's a tiger, whaddaya say? Aw, man, whatever, you big freak. Go ahead home with Rocky. See how much fun you can have in bed when you both wanna keep your jeans on."

"Are you looking at my girl? What, you think she's a lezzie, too? Back the fuck up, man, and don't let me catch you looking at her again. You hear me? Don't make me have to come over there and fuck with you, dyke. Don't think I won't. Just walk away from her."

"Mommy, what is it?"

HIGH-HEELED SHOES

On my nineteenth birthday, I meet a punk-rock femme with black hair rinsed midnight blue who comes on to me at my party over near the pool table by running her fingernails down the front panels of my sleeveless leather shirt and asking, "What's under here?" Thinking she's asking me undergarment questions, I reply, "Nothing," and she takes hold of it at the top and unsnaps it all the way down, showing my breasts, belly, and rising flush of excitement. I stand still while she gives me a long look, smiles, and says, "Doesn't look like nothing to me."

We started dating, spending long hours on the ancient futon in her claptrap apartment and, when we could no longer stand her roommates' fighting anymore, going out. She wore her power as a femme like a mantle, like a snake draped around her neck, always ready for her, always warning me, and I loved the crackle of her. She liked to get dressed up, and she made me snort and paw the ground in some of the outfits she strolled out in when I came to pick her up in my old blue Chevy. Short skirts or, even better, long skirts slit far up the side. Corset tops, blouses that were made entirely out of gauze and mesh, things with buckles and straps, snaps and straps, everything black, gray, and silver over fishnets or seamed stockings. It was my job to straighten the seams. Mostly she wore boots on these outings. Heavy ones, nearly knee high, and I loved the contrast, her lithe frame and girly clothes topped by a short fluff of primary-colored hair and finishing with some steel-toed, don't-fuck-with-me boots.

But one day she came out in high heels. They seemed very

high to me at the time, but were probably only three inches or so. I had never seen them before. Bedroom shoes is how I thought of them, a prop dug up from somewhere for an exciting night of playing at something I'd be hearing about presently. I assumed their appearance to be a sign that we were not, in fact, going much of anyplace, which seemed like a perfectly fine idea to me. Especially after I got a glimpse of her calves in those heels, suddenly looking like they were made to wrap around the bulk of me. But she got her coat, and I balked.

"You're wearing those?" I asked. "Out?"

She looked at me very strangely, and said "Yes, that's the plan," in the kind of extrapatient voice one uses with a small child. In that moment, a fear I had never felt before shot through my heart.

We lived in a tiny, safe, liberal, and enlightened city. Violent crime was low, police presence was high, and queers were everywhere. But suddenly all I could see in those shoes was danger; they rang in my heart like shiny black Klaxons. I couldn't stop thinking about what might happen if there was Trouble. The Ghost of Women's Studies Past rose up in my panicked chest and started doing a warning chorus of "high-heeled shoes are a device created by men to keep women vulnerable."

I saw visions of myself not being able to keep her safe, not being able to keep the wolves at bay long enough for her to get far enough in three-inch spikes to keep herself safe. Whether she might call for help never crossed my mind, nor did how I might fare. In that moment, all I could see or hear was the horrible potential for her, if I couldn't be big enough, strong enough: How could she get away, in those shoes? How could she protect herself, in those shoes?

I was very stupid when I was nineteen, too stupid to confess all of this to her, maybe because I didn't want to seem like I was afraid to tangle with trouble if I had to, maybe because I didn't know how to explain it all, or maybe for some other reason that the intervening years have mercifully washed away. But I asked her not to go out in them, making some kind of hop-along excuse so I wouldn't have to confess my blinding fear of not being strong enough to protect her if I had to.

She agreed with a strange tone in her voice, and it wasn't until I was much older and substantially less stupid that I understood that my silence about my own fear had shamed her. She thought I didn't like her high heels, that I thought she or they were unattractive or foolish. I understand now that she had taken a lot of care to get dressed up for my delectation, and that I had ruined my surprise and her pleasure with my inability to tell her what the real problem was. To this day the regret of it stays fresh in the cool cupboards of my mind.

Later, after we ended it, she took up with a butch who encouraged her high-heel habits and laughed at me for my stupidity, which I probably deserved. I just couldn't get past the images in my mind that seemed so dangerous, and after-the-fact protestations that I only had her best interest in mind sounded as lame as you might expect. All I could see was my crumpled body and her delicate throat, encircled by a brawny malfeasant's arm.

It didn't occur to me that she might step out of them and go barefoot through the streets, or use them as better weapons than I carried, or that she could aim a high-kick in those shoes sure to take a cruel divot out of any miscreant stupid enough to think like my women's studies professor. All I knew was that protecting her was my job, maybe even more my job than loving her was, that keeping her safe was my sacred butch trust, and I wasn't sure I could do it. I wasn't sure I could be big enough, smart enough, or mean enough, wasn't sure I had the heart for it, or the balls. I understood all of a sudden the older butches I knew who were so hard, so hardened by life, so quick to see every slight and slow to welcome any joy, and I went home later and sat up all night, wondering if I would have to become them in order to be able someday to walk out the door with a beautiful girl in high-heeled shoes and not be afraid.

MY BUTCH BROTHERS

We stand hip-to-hip, in half circles around anything that can be stood around. We laugh too loud, and we smoke, and we laugh some more, in our little tribes, my brothers and I: we stand around the grill, or the open hood of a car, or a set of stairs, or a girl, and we tease each other and talk and make dirty jokes and innuendo and we laugh, because for fucking once there are enough of us that we're safe no matter who takes exception to our gender, our performance. So we can take up as much space as we want, and we do.

We call each other when things are tough, our voices tight, clipped: Dude. Not good. Can you meet me? And when we meet we rinse whatever's bad away with tequila, or we speak it into a case of glasses and smash each one, or we scream it out the windows of a car going too fast on a twisting farm road, or we say it softly to our hands, with a shrug, between "How was I supposed to know?" and "Well? What can you do?" and the brotherhood listens and we shake our heads and we hold our brother when ze cries. We walk every day along a line between being ready to put our bodies and our blood between any threat and any brother, and trying to help each of us grow strong enough so that's not necessary. Not that we wouldn't show up, but if we couldn't. That happens.

They're all paying attention to my girl, my family, even when I'm not looking, or not there to see. They're all making sure everyone has what she or he needs and that my wife isn't getting pawed by some numbnuts over by the bar while she's just trying to have an innocent drink and chat with Dan, and they're quietly keeping an eye on Ryan to make sure he's not doing the bad thing he isn't supposed to do again. They are extensions of me in ways that make me feel so safe and so loved. They're seeing everything else with my eyes as well as theirs because they know me, they know what worries me and delights me, they know what I know.

I am so grateful for them, for their wonderful hearts and for their solid protection. As a very young butch, my best friend was another young butch named Chief, and we used to make jokes about how many people it would take in a fight before we were outnumbered. We were cocky and stupid, but we also knew that either of us—both disinclined to fight, both calm and gentle souls—would have killed or died to protect the other without ever counting the cost. It was with Chief that I learned what it meant to have a friend for the first time, a friend who I could trust not only with my secrets but with my life, not only with my life but with the lives of my loved ones.

Years later when I married, I asked Chief to hold one corner of our *chuppah*, the ceremonial canopy under which a Jewish couple is married that signifies their home. The people who hold the *chuppah* are supposed to be those who one trusts to guard the *shalom bayit*, the peace of that house. We chose the people for a variety of reasons, but Chief was and is the one who really symbolizes that feeling of safety for me; ze is still the first one I think of to call when there's a crisis.

A couple of years later, when we met Tori, we knew her for the same kind of a thing and brought her close. For a while it was like having a littler brother, a madcap scapegrace who always needed minding, but after a while it wasn't like that anymore. Tori balanced the three of us at least as often as she unbalanced us, and I found myself sometimes telling her things a little too tender, a little too uncertain, to tell Chief. In the wedding photos there's Tori too, on the other side of the *chuppah* from Chief, alternating between looking like she'll burst from the pride of her office and making faces at Chief across the way. Tori seemed then, and still seems, like the safety of my house in the meaning of my family, my descendant line. Since I may not have heirs of my own, and if I do they're not likely to be queer, Tori is the one into whom I have poured my sense of tribe because she has always been the one who believed in it as much as I do. In her reposes my defense against my ideals dying with me, and she is the first one I think of to call when I am feeling useless.

It feels like the flying wedge, having these brothers. The flying wedge was a football play from the early days, in which players linked arms and, in a V-shape like geese, ran downfield, protecting a single runner with the ball just behind the point of the V, getting him safely over the goal line through their sheer numbers and inertia. Though they've outlawed it in football, I can see very clearly those moments in which I was protected by the wedge of my butch brothers, them heedless to their own injury and me running headlong and unafraid for the goal line.

There have been fights and fallings-out. Fights over girls and moments of disrespect, fights over all sorts of things, all disguises for the fighting we wish we could do against the world that we turn on one another instead. But like brothers, like family, we fight and make up, and even if we haven't quite managed to make up yet we know it's out there, waiting, shimmering in the distance. It never feels like no, to me, just like not quite yet. In a world of so little certainty and even less stability, the force and weight and warmth of my brothers, even the ones I don't see anymore, even the ones I haven't met yet, keeps me safe enough to do what I am afraid to do. I hope I am doing the same for them. They all deserve it.

My desire in this moment, more than anything, is to name them all, all the butches of my life who have been my brothers: Dori and Carmen and Jess and Chris and Chief and Tori, J and Ren and Ryan and Cody and KJ and Ty, Sasha and Andy and Turner and Gunner and Ivan. My brothers, then and now. Thank you.

CROSSING THE STREET

1. Crossing the street with Kate, on the way back from the latest dinner in more than ten years of friendship, after dark. She's taken my arm, her hand warm on me even through my shirt, holding tight, pressed hip-to-hip to keep the secrets shared at dinner safe between us, in the shade of me. We reach a construction barrier, and there's only room for one body at a time along the curb. I take her hand in my left, place it in my right, hold it at the level of my heart and promenade her before me through the narrow walkway, matching her long, even step until there's room for the both of us again, and I reverse the movement, putting her hand back in the crook of my arm and holding it there. She looks at me, eyes brimming with recognition and happiness, and I am seen, known, approved of and the source of her delight. In the moment, it is all I have ever wanted to be.

2. Crossing the street with Robert, the next morning on the way to the first breakfast of a new acquaintance, he leans heavily on his cane after half a block, places his feet with care, and chats bravely as we go on about the wonders of his mechanic. We reach the cross street, four lanes of fast traffic, and instinctively I cross behind him to put myself between him and the oncoming cars, him on my lee side, just in case, and he says, when I reappear at his right elbow, "Ah, the guard position," and then, a full beat later, "Thank you." He sounds slightly surprised and more than a little pleased, understanding without a word everything I have

just said about how I understand my identity, about the dynamic between us, about my desire.

3. Crossing the street alone, after lunch that afternoon, I get nearly all the way to the other curb when I see her, still beginning across slowly, unsteadily, also with a cane. I ask in my best goodboy tones, "Would you like me to help you across?" and she sighs gratefully and puts her arm through mine unquestioningly, saying only, "I wish you'd come along two blocks ago." We walk slowly across the street, small steps, and a brawny assist up the curb with no cutout, while traffic queues up at a green light. When we're safely across, she pats my arm and tells me I'm a nice boy, that the world needs more young men like me, and although I've been more helpful on this street than on either of the others, I'm invisible to her, and it shows me in the bright California sun exactly what I am.

HAIR

There's a photo of me that I think of as The Last Kid Photo, one taken just before I was sent off for my first perm and all the nonsense that came with it. I am in Ms. Miller's seventh grade social studies class, wearing a green sweater with a B on it, B for Benetton, a brand I learned about from the much more sartorially sophisticated girls with whom I went to summer camp, but which Ms. Miller always used to say was for Bergman. My hair is long and stick straight, hanging down to the middle of my back. I am slightly more or less than eight months away from my Bat Mitzvah, and it is time—my mother informs me—to start planning. In October, I will be standing up in front of nearly everyone I have known well in my life to read from the Torah and make my entrance into Jewish society as an adult. To do this, I will have to look appropriately womanly, which requires a program of preparation including hair, earrings, dress shopping, and so on. Hair first.

At the salon, Gina (my *stylist*) asks me what I want. I do not know. I don't want anything much, really, I am perfectly happy with my hair as it is, but I know that's not the right answer. It is the late eighties, and hair with a lot of volume is *in*. Hair that requires maintenance, and tools, and prayer for dry days. My mother starts to outline her vision of my hair, which makes very little sense to me as she explains it, despite the fact that she has talked about it with me more than once, and I have nodded along as though I understood. Layers are to be employed, and a permanent wave. I'm still nodding. I have no idea what I'm in for. They try to get me to take off my shirt and wrap myself in a funny little smock, but I refuse. I am not taking off my clothes at the hairdresser's. My mother, tight-lipped, shrugs.

An hour later, I am still in this chair. My hair has been washed and cut, and rolled onto what seem like thousands of little rollers of various sizes while I hand Gina an endless succession of little squares of tissue paper and she yanks my hair hard, over and over again, in order to work it into all of these little rolls. It takes forever, and there are frequent work stoppages so that she and my mother can talk about things I don't really understand. I sit and am worked on, passively allowing myself to be turned this way and that, responding to instructions to sit up straighter, tilt my chin up or down, look left or right. All the while Gina's coral-tipped hand reaching forward endlessly for more of those little squares of paper. At length, she says, "All right!" and I am delighted, I want to be finished, I am hungry and I need to pee.

Then she wraps cotton batting, which itches terribly, along the outline of the million rollers in my hair, tells me to tilt my head way back, and not breathe in too much if I can avoid it. Before I can say, "What!?" her hand is hard on my forehead, forcing my head back far enough, and she is dousing my tender, assaulted skin with chemicals that sting on contact. When I yelp, she says, "I know," and keeps pouring, the fumes choking me and my tormented scalp burning, while she and my mother chat away. When I tell them that it hurts, that I feel sick, they say, with great sympathy, that yes, it's not too pleasant, is it? They don't stop.

There's another round of caustic liquid, then a smelly half hour under a dryer, then the harvesting of the tiny plastic rollers, thank G-d, and then the rinsing of my head under cool water, which is an incredible relief. I am so glad to be finished, I could cry. I start to shrug out of my plastic smock.

We're not done. Now it's time for more cutting, and then blowing dry, more instructions not to breathe, to shield my eyes with my hand, to look up or down or away. By the time it's all finished, more than three hours later, I am handed back my glasses and told to look at myself in the mirror, which I do. It seems to me in that moment that a spitting cobra has taken up residence on my head, curling malevolently over my forehead, hood puffed around my ears. In the mirror, my mother is smiling hugely. I smile, too.

The next morning, after I get out of the shower, I am confronted with a head of curly hair. I have never had curly hair before, but I don't think much of it. I brush it a bit, as I tend to do, then get dressed and go downstairs for breakfast. When she sees me, my mother is displeased and disbelieving. What, she wants to know, is the rat's nest on my head? Why have I not styled it?

"I didn't know I was supposed to," I reply meekly.

The look she gives me, full of love and despair, is one I will come to be very familiar with before my teenaged years are over. She leads me upstairs and shows me how to rouse the cobra on my head again, which also makes me late for school, so she drives me and I miss chorus.

Over the next six years, there are quarterly perms. I become adept at styling my hair at a variety of levels of industriousness, from Full Battle Coiffure for the High Holidays and family events, a process requiring an aerosolized can of AquaNet, a round brush, and a blow-dryer fitter with a diffuser that makes it look like a microphone from the early days of radio, to a sort of slapdash, indifferent hairstyle that requires little more than getting my bangs out of my eyes and giving the rest a little fluff and tease with my fingers. It is clear to me, even then, that this is a fake-it-till-you-make-it kind of a gesture for my mother; that she is convinced that there is a stylish young lady someplace inside me and that I just need to let her come to the fore.

It makes sense to her; she was a stylish young lady at my age and is a gorgeous, youthful, stylish woman now: small framed, green-eyed like me, with glossy chestnut hair rich with natural highlights, beautifully dressed, displaying the latest proof of my father's affection for her in increasing weight of gold and sapphires. Perhaps, she thinks, I am just a little awkward. Perhaps I will blossom any minute now, if the right combination of makeup and jewelry and hair and clothing can be applied.

She is searching for it, and I am wearing the results as best I can manage. I wear most of them on my head, always feeling faintly ridiculous, like a white man in a ceremonial headpiece he bought for cash from the indigenous people wherever he vacationed and is now showing off in his living room back home. Femininity and the stuff of it, from my hairstyle to my blue eyeshadow, crazy earrings to purple fingernails, feels like someplace I don't know the customs of and where I can only shuffle along, out of step, my feet stomping past the drought while everyone else's are calling rain.

In my first year of college, Bill Clinton got elected president and the next day, in a hopeful mood, I found someone to cut off all my hair. I had no idea, again, what I wanted so I just sat down in the chair and said that I was done, really finished, with having long hair. The amiable woman to whom I said it nodded and gestured at the level of the top of my ears, asking if that would be a good length. It seemed a terrifying length. I had never in my entire life had hair that short; even as a scapegrace five-year-old fond of eating my lunch under the deck I had maintained a long ponytail. I nodded dumbly, took off my glasses, and shut my eyes.

When she asked, "Should I buzz this?" I nodded again, and murmured a quiet prayer. I heard the clippers chatter to life, and breathed out a long breath while heaps of my hair settled softly to the floor around me. At length, the hairdresser bid me to open my eyes and, when I put my glasses on, I was struck by the extraordinary sensation of liking the look of the person looking back at me for the first time since I could remember. Afterward, I paid and walked out, and the cold late-fall wind bit into the damp back of my shorn neck. It hurt, and I laughed.

The recipient of your handkerchief may want to keep it, as a token of the kindness. Be glad. Ze will leave with a tangible reminder of the idea that there are people in the world who are willing to go to a little extra trouble in order to take care of those around them. A day in which you have seeded the world with this idea is a good day.

BEING AN ASSHOLE

I meet hir on a Sunday night at karaoke, a short and handsome butch in hir early twenties, buzz cut and squared away in blue jeans and a black T-shirt, small and neat and wearing a smile halfway between a snicker and a leer. Someone introduces us, and we start talking, me and this butch, standing at the bar and having a drink while a girl I don't know fumbles her way through a Melissa Etheridge ballad in that way that suggests that she's just now noticed that singing along in the car isn't exactly the same thing as singing it by herself. Still, you know, karaoke can accept all things. Then the butch says, "She should just stand there and let us look at her tits." And I think, oh, here we go again.

Okay, I got lucky. I had great femme mentors, I had good role models of gentle men, I found ways to be a butch that did not require being an ass in public, ways of masculinity that were not misogyny—which is what I see more often than I used to these days, this way of butches distancing themselves from any and all things feminine by embodying the worst excesses of men, from relatively harmless ones like spitting on the street and wearing too much cheap cologne to behaving as though women were an entirely separate species of second-class citizen, the objects of jokes and derision.

It turns my stomach every time, makes me want to scream every time, these embodiments, from people who have cunts themselves, whatever they call them these days, and were raised and socialized as women no matter how little they felt that really described them, and therefore should bloody well know better, of the notion that all things female or feminine are weak, silly, and easily disregarded.

It's pushing back, is what it is. It's finally getting out of your parents' house, out from under their supervision and checkbook and bullshit about being a girl, and striking out on your own, all full of promise and self-determination. It starts with leaving everything girly in your closet at home and packing only the jeans and T-shirts. It's buying underwear on your own for the first time and standing there in the aisle at the store with the package that has the kind you usually got and thinking the hell with that, and getting what you want. It's noticing how much more comfortable it is to sit with your feet planted wide, knees apart, when no one's sniping at you to sit like a lady, it's feeling the last of your hair fall to the floor in the barber shop, it's the soaring freedom of shedding whatever tied you to a girlhood you never wanted, never liked, were never really convinced was yours and not someone else's, and taking those first few unencumbered steps forward as a butch, the cool breeze or a warm hand playing with the newly sensitive spot on the back of your neck and thinking, *Finally*. Fucking finally.

Stop there. Don't go any further. Let go of all the femininity that was ever imposed upon you, cast it away and walk upright for the first time, but going further isn't going to make it better for you. This is the same theory that suggests that if planting a bulb six inches deep is good, planting it a foot deep is better. It isn't. Distance matters, especially when it's a matter of distance from the sun.

Leave femininity aside, but don't ruin it. Think of it like a castoff piece of clothes, fold it gently and leave it out where some young thing who wants it can pick it up. Imagine, just for a minute, a young thing raised the reverse of you but longing all his young life for exactly what you hated. Imagine him picking up the femininity that you sloughed off and taking it home with great glee and breathless anticipation, putting it on in the mirror when no one's home, smoothing it over himself, smiling shyly at his reflection, thinking about being asked to dance.

And then walk tall, and do your best. Don't spit and make blonde jokes and condescend to femmes. Don't spend all that energy to determine your own gender expression only to climb blindly into the worst excesses of doltish man-ness. Even when you make mistakes—and oh, you will—even when you do things that make the femmes in your life sigh exasperated sighs or grit their teeth together in frustration, at least let them have come from places of good intention.

Hold your great esteem for the power of femmes close to your heart while you forge your own way (and if you do not have this great esteem, sit at the feet of powerful femmes until you develop some). Let it include everything you need and most of what you want, be a hearty blend of every good quality you've ever seen in anyone whose gender delights you. Learn when to be gentle and when to be strong; straighten your tie and shine your shoes and be a credit to yourself, and a credit to the tribe.

WHAT A BUTCH MAY USE

1. I keep a fountain pen in my pocket, full of green ink; snotty though you may think it is to collect something like fountain pens, I am nevertheless a writer. Though writers today are really more typists than people who indulge in an act of actual writing and perhaps need a new name, we still do write, or at least I do. I jot down notes with my fountain pen, I sign things with it, I use it to write postcards so that my friends across the country know at a glance which card is from me by the bold stroke of my shoddy penmanship made grand with emerald ink and a good nib. Carrying a Bic gets the job done, but the fountain pen gives it style, a little bit of Bond, and makes you stand out as someone who takes care with the details, makes people think you're the kind of butch who not only won't forget flowers but will know to trim the stems with the kitchen shears under running water and then put them in a vase with an aspirin you bring in your suitcoat pocket while she puts the finishing touches on her ensemble, but will not try to arrange them in any way. It seems like the kind of thing that goes with a basic understanding of the waltz, the stock market, the combustion engine, or all three, like the sort of an item purchased and used by a butch who will not lose your number, who will call when ze says ze will, and who will never, ever leave you hanging on call waiting, who has in fact disabled call waiting, in case you call. The fountain pen belongs to the hopeless throwback, the romantic individual, the one who has *Miss Manners' Guide to Life* around the house and isn't afraid to use it.

2. In my pants pocket is a pocketknife, always; a modest battered little silver one I picked up at a flea market for four dollars and had sharpened down the row for a buck by a man named Buck, not coincidentally I imagine, and it gets a lot of use. You never know how frequently a pocketknife could come in handy until you start carrying one and realize that you have it out a dozen times a day, that someone nearby is practically always struggling to rip or tear something open with teeth, keys, fingernails, the back of an earring or bare hands, and that a butch with a pocketknife can slide it out of hir pocket, open it, and hand it over, handle first. A butch with a pocketknife—not a candy-assed French brand that can't tolerate the oils of skin but an old workhorse that can be used to slice cheese, cardboard, rope, or anything else—and who is willing to let others use it probably also has jumper cables for you, and a spare dry sweatshirt that's likely to fit, and will be perfectly happy and in fact quietly pleased to put on a jacket and shoes and go out and drive ten miles in the rain at night because you think you might like to have a slice of lemon pie, and will also remember that you like a glass of warm vanilla milk with it and will make sure that ze picks some milk up on the way home against the possibility that you might happen to be out. The pocketknife belongs to the butch who deals in practicalities, in service, in capacity rather than intention, and if this butch cannot fix your wiring then ze will arrange to have it done for you while you're at work one day, and think of this as a romantic surprise, which it is.

3. I wear cufflinks, which I consider a harmless affectation on my part. I wear them one pair at a time with my plain shirts and my heavy silk ties, a little bit of pizazz at the ends of my sleeves.

I consider them as I dress because I want to make sure my cufflinks match my mood, that they have the same feel as the outfit
and the outing, and girls coo appreciatively over them, fondle
my french cuffs and smile, take my hands and hold them up so
that they can see my cufflinks. I shop for these, sometimes at the
same time I shop for jewelry for girls of my acquaintance, and for
ties and socks and other accessories of life, things I use to make
myself look sharp for dates, to convey that the extra step of care
has been taken in my appearance. Buttoned cuffs are certainly
perfectly serviceable, and if you remember to button your gaunt-
let button you're well on your way for sure, but a butch who wears
cufflinks knows how to shop for jewelry and will present you with
the loveliest, most surprising things; ze will understand that you
have seventeen pairs of black silk trousers and why. A butch who
wears cufflinks will happily sit for an hour in hir underwear on
the sofa, reading, until you say, "Okay, sweetie, I'm almost ready,"
whereupon ze knows it is time for hir to dress in five minutes and
get out of the way again, fastening hir cufflinks in the kitchen
and tying hir tie in the reflection of the television and holding
the right coat out for you when you appear from the bathroom, a
vision of beauty, ready to leave. The cufflinks belong to the butch
who will buy you a scarf that matches either your eyes or your
very favorite sweater exactly, and present it as merely the wrapping for another, more interesting, smaller box that turns out to
contain something thoroughly delightful—maybe a lemondrop,
maybe a butterfly, maybe an engagement ring.

FEMME FOR DUMMIES

I am aware that there are many butches who are attracted to, partner with, and live with butches, boys, and men. I think that this is a perfectly lovely idea (I have, in fact, done each of the above at least once), and if you have any extra closet space at your house, please let me know. You will not be getting any shit from me. Feel free to skip. Nevertheless, there is a certain body of information that may be very useful to femme-oriented butches— hints, tips, that sort of thing—when it comes to learning the secrets of femmes. I learned these secrets through a combination of generous elder femmes, keen observation of the species (with careful attention to the many subspecies), and a great number of very bad mistakes. In an effort to assist younger butches of the femme-admiring persuasion with their efforts in wooing, and then pleasing, the femmes in their lives, and as a way of honoring the femmes I love by making their lives perhaps a little nicer, I thought I would set down a little of what I know. *Salvete*, fellas, and best of luck to you.

ON FEMMES AND COMPORTMENT
1. Femmes are not defined by their clothes, hair, or makeup. Not all femmes are inclined toward superfeminine clothing. Do not be surprised when you meet a girl and get all types of marvelous femme signals from her even though she's wearing jeans and a pullover and Birkenstocks, even if she shows no interest in makeup. Although I would make a sizable bet that you'll find a matched set of lingerie under there.

2. That being said, many femmes are interested and invested in their clothes, makeup, hair, nails, or some combination thereof. Many femmes have large wardrobes, great bags full of confusing cosmetic items, stacks and stacks of shoes, a rainbow of nail polish colors. And mousse, and gel, and hairspray, which do not, I have it on excellent authority, serve the same function. Warning: Do not make the mistake of thinking that a femme's interest in Estée Lauder is incompatible with great intelligence, or you will miss many pleasures of life. Not the least of which is the company of femmes.

3. Remember that you like it when the femme in your life is dressed up, looking spiffed up with coordinating everything. Even if you don't much care, remember that *she* likes it. If the femme of your heart is of this variety, remember it when she asks you to accompany her to the mall or shoe store. On the other hand, there's no reason you can't bring a book or a radio on which you can tune in your favorite music or sporting event, park yourself in the husband chair, let the sales staff bring all the different sizes and colors, and only pay attention at the actual moment of "Honey? What do you think?" No reason to be a martyr about it.

4. "Does this make me look fat?" is a question that butches quail to hear, and for good reason. Most girls, living as we do in this *Cosmo* culture, think that looking fat is a bad thing and they attempt to avoid it wherever possible. (For the record, I know some who don't and they are without exception sexy as hell. I will leave the cultural critique of body image for someone who knows more about it than I do, but please do bear in mind that fat is not always

considered by a girl to be a bad thing, and thank G-d for that. You, buster, had damn well better be sure how your girl feels about it before you open your mouth. But, moving on.) Attention, butches. This is not an essay question. There are only two possible answers, reproduced here to make your life easier:

    * (If it doesn't) "Of course not."
    * (If it does) "That [item] is not cut very well."

Remember—the fault is in the garment, certainly not the girl. There is nothing whatsoever wrong with the shape of her. Some designers cut their clothes for certain body types and others for others. Occasionally the pattern will make her ass look strangely square or the fabric will cling in an unflattering way, but Not Cut Well is always the answer, and it has the extremely delightful quality of saving your ass and being completely true at the same time. Use it wisely.

5. Many femmes have extensive collections of at least one item of clothing or jewelry; shoes, handbags, and earrings seem to be the most popular, but scarves, cardigan sweaters, little hats, jeans, and just about everything else have been recorded. Now hear this: there is no way to say that you think she has enough of this item, no way to keep her from buying more, and no way to prevent your clothes getting slowly squashed closer to your end of the closet. Even if you wanted to, which, on further reflection, I think you'll find that you really, in your heart of hearts, don't. Go down to the basement, build her a rack for whatever it is, and be happy.

6. She will always look cuter in your clothes than you do. Even if she is a substantially different size and all she can really wear of yours is your socks, they will still look cuter on her. What's more, you will experience a strange rush of joy every time you see her in them.

ON FEMMES AND SEX

1. Butch and Femme are not synonymous with Top and Bottom. There are Femme Tops, Butch Bottoms, and switches on both sides of the aisle. Many femmes enjoy taking charge in the bedroom or shower, or sofa, or cheap motel, or alleyway, or romantic bluff, back porch, et cetera, from time to time or on a regular basis. There's nothing wrong with that, just as there's nothing wrong with it if she doesn't want to be on top. A willingness to be flexible about certain butch/femme sexual assumptions will often go a long way toward making a femme happy in bed. Besides, no matter what you get up to there's no need to worry about your reputation. A femme will never tell.

2. New shoes can absolutely count as a sex toy in a femme's mind. It is the wise butch who remembers this.

3. It will serve you a great deal better in the long run to pay attention to the subtle signals your femme may be sending than to stick with one tried-and-true way of initiating sex. Just because you know she always loves a long, lazy Saturday morning snuggle that turns slowly into a sweaty romp doesn't mean that you are imagining the glint in her eyes as she walks off, completely naked, to fold the laundry. (I am not trying to suggest that folding the laundry is a femme's exclusive province. I just chose it as an

activity that tends to feature a certain amount of bending over. Feel free to substitute weeding, swapping out the spark plugs in the old Rambler, laying tile in the front hallway, or whatever suits your girl. Woman. Whichever she prefers).

4. Sometimes femmes who are experiencing cramps or other associated menstrual discomfort will welcome a few quick orgasms for the sake of pain relief. Sometimes you will be much better off going across the street for Pringles, a Baby Ruth, and a few Boston Cream doughnuts. The correct query is: Sweetheart, I'd be happy to do whatever would help you feel happier or more comfortable. Is there anything you can think of? Practice in front of the mirror until you can say it with only the merest hint of sexual innuendo, or there's every possibility that you'll lose credit for the nice thought and get yelled at to stop always thinking about sex, get away from her, and go across the street for chocolate-covered pretzels and canned pears.

5. You should be prepared, especially at the early stages of a courtship, to discover that your femme can produce a wider range of sensation in your body with a smoldering glance and her soft palm on your thigh through your jeans than you can in hers with all the toys you've got in that drawer beside your bed. There are two lessons in this: First—sometimes less really is more. Second—a femme will have her way with you when she wants to. These two lessons form the foundation of any successful butch's understanding of femme sexuality, and remembering them will keep you out of trouble at least half the time.

The other half of the time, you're on your own, bubba.

Look away while your handkerchief is used. Don't watch it as though it were a precious thing you are worried about the welfare of in someone else's hand; let it be used as thoroughly and unselfconsciously as it needs to be. The item is only a scrap of cloth, only a vessel of care, of which there will always be more from you.

WHEN I'M FAR FROM HOME

As a kid, I was told and understood that the Jews of the world were a great tribe, spanning geography and the fullness of time, a single people with a common heart, and that should I ever find myself far from home, lost, hopeless or in need, I should turn myself in to the nearest synagogue and I would be kept safe within my tribe. I imagined myself traveling, making my ragged way to a synagogue, and being welcomed in and cared for. I always found it incredibly comforting, and having what felt like a worldwide safety net, a refuge even in the metaphorical desert, made the great unknown seem like a much safer place. It made me fearless in the face of the unknown, made me feel as though anywhere I had never been was waiting for me.

Although I understand now in a way I did not when I was twelve the global politics that complicate the issue, I'm sure it's more or less still true. These days, though, my traveling mercies are the gifts of femmes. My hands, my gaze, my walk and my manner, the referent of my eyes, mark me as a butch who appreciates femmes, who honors and cherishes and delights in them, and when I am away from my wife, my home, other femmes soothe me as though it were as much my birthright as my religion.

I've just been away from home, a week without my adored wife, and the girls are keeping an eye on me. At brunch, little Dani piles her coat, her scarf, and her bag onto my uncomplaining lap; she gives me instructions about her omelette so I can order for her while she visits the little femmes room; she sends me on an errand, all with the unconscious ease and love of a girl who knows me for a butch, not a stereotype but a phenotype, and honors me.

Barbara preens me before photos, sending me to get my suit jacket, emptying my pockets of unsightly items and brushing me free of lint while Kate breathes on and then smoothes my hair, tugs my cuffs, holds my hand. Sarah Grace leans back against me in our group photo, between my wide-planted feet and my hands instead of her own butch's enclosure, showing me she knows she's safe as a vault with me, that if she was far, lost, or in need she could always find comfort from me, her beloved's brother in this honorable, diminishing but undimmed fraternity of butch.

My wife asks me to please thank them, these girls and women who soothe and smooth and allow me to give the honorable service of a butch, to have these moments of home away from home. She knows that without these women to ground and heal me I slip away a little bit; that all of them, all of you, cherished and adored, keep me safe until I get home.

FAGGOT BUTCH

"I hated that essay," he says to me, "about femmes who care for you when you travel; I really hated it." And when I ask why he tells me that he thinks it sounds like all butches should be soothed by femmes, and vice versa; he says, "Why would those femmes have assumed that you were a butch who liked femmes?" He says, "Maybe you're a faggot butch, did they even consider that?" He says, "I know you're not just for femmes."

That's what he says, but I know what he's thinking. And even though I know how dangerous it is to assume I know what someone is thinking, I know this butch maybe as well as I know myself, and he's thinking, "Fuck you, for having it easy even in being queer. Fuck you for going along on your happy little way to San Francisco and finding a bunch of femmes who see you as a big stud-duck butch and just want to pour themselves through your fingers. It's just as hard to be a faggot butch as it is to be any kind of fag."

There's all that masculinity to consider when you want to rub up against someone, like that old joke about porcupines:

How do porcupines mate?

Very carefully.

He's saying, "I want to show up at brunch someplace and assume that anyone who I want to flirt with will want to flirt back, and will do it, will want to, without fear of recrimination from hir community. I want you to put something in that book of yours for me. I am a butch whose identity, sexual or otherwise, has nothing to do with femmes. They are not my natural partners in this gender crime the way they are yours. I wake and sleep in the arms of butches like me, butches who understand a whole host of things about my life, my world, the way I see things, the way things affect me that no one else could understand. Write about us. Write that we have sweet, hot sex in which no one has to put on a pair of panties, or take them off; write about how good it feels when ze fucks me hard, so hard. Write about how it feels to fall asleep with the weight of a butch on you, one tattooed arm and one furry leg pinning you down and grounding you in your sleep.

"Write about all the ways in which butches care for each other, comfort each other. Write about how we understand all the shit that comes in the world for our partners and salve it as best we can, about how I have all the more respect for hir because of all I know it takes to survive as a butch.

"Write about how, as soon as butches were no longer the scourge of dykedom for aping masculinity, or whatever that baloney was, it became faggot butches who were scorned and derided. Everyone understands butch/femme because it seems familiar, like Ozzie and Harriet but with better hair and more pussy. Everyone understands femme on femme, even though you don't see it all that often cause it doesn't read queer, you know, but it's in the first images of 'lesbian love' most of us see, in porn or on television. Two longhaired pretty girls smooching in a daring fashion wherever they happen to be. No one's threatened by that, not the dykes, not the men, nobody, but if I want to kiss my butch anywhere, I'd better be damn sure of my audience, or better yet, be sure we don't have one.

"I can be a butch without opening doors for girls," he's saying.

"I can do it even if I follow while dancing, I can do it without spending my Saturday afternoons as a femme's shopping bottom at the mall and I do. I am. I am honorable, I take good care of the people I love as well as I possibly can; I watch out for my community. I have a butch heart full of love that I can express when I feel safe enough; I walk in the world resisting gender norms and transgressing gender rules, transcending them. I am fixing whatever I can, whenever I can, and I laugh, and play, and let the spaces in my masculinity show, just like you, just like every butch. I get all slicked up for a date in a suit and tie and I pick up my date, also in a suit and tie, and we just open the door if we get to it first and we take turns paying, and it doesn't make me less a butch. It doesn't make me less of anything. It doesn't mean that I don't think femmes are swell, I surely do, but they are not my salvation when I travel, they are not the North of my heart's compass. That's butches for me, and I will always go a little weak when I see someone who looks scared and hardened and delighted and ashamed and proud—proud, just like me.

"You're writing a book? Of course, I'm glad, but don't chicken out. Don't write a book that speaks so many volumes about your adoration for femmes that it leaves out the ways in which I know you cherish butches too. Yes, not the same way as you cherish femmes, entirely differently, butches and femmes are different creatures, sure, but I don't just mean how glad you are and always will be to have butch brothers, a butch tribe. I mean, make sure you don't forget to mention that you put butches on their knees in front of you and enjoy them, that you kneel down too, that you sit sometimes stunned by how much you want to lick a buzz cut or a hot tattoo, that you know what a great grace it is to fall asleep next to a butch's heart and muscle and skin and ink and fur, that you understand how wonderful it can be to feel butch arms around you. Make sure you mention me, make sure you give me and my lovers and my life the same benefit of some of your words, make sure you don't write another book that leaves us on the cutting-room floor. Give us a place on the landscape, help us become visible. Say this: Say that when butches love butches they hold lightning between them, but that as much as it burns it also illuminates. That it's the sweetest burn I've ever known in my life of searing pain, that it keeps me from feeling the flames of the world's hate licking the soles of my boots, that I hold it in my heart and it fuels me every day. Say that it shows me things I could never see any other way, that without it I would grow cold and die. Say that there is nothing else I would rather be."

WHAT THE STONE IS MADE OF

You could chew off a leg to get out of a trap and still be faster on three legs than most dogs are on four but for a little hitch in your stride. You grow, slow, toward survival, around any incursion, reminding me always of the trees I have seen encompass the barbed wire wrapped around their trunks. It must bite, at first, to strain against such a thing. I know that trees don't have nervous systems, but even so, on the cellular level, some phytological imperative in them understands that leaving the open gouges to the mercy of weather and bugs is a bad survival strategy, so it hurts itself more in order to survive. You do the same thing.

We grow around every injury, never able to heal it—we just encompass it. We take every ache, every hurt, every shame into ourselves and live with it inside our skins. Is it this that becomes our stone?

It makes sense. It feels like a rock in my gut, still, when someone is mean to me or hurts the feelings I am not supposed to have to be hurt. I don't show it. Maybe I am only supporting an untenable myth with my stoicism, but in my injury the last thing I want to do is find the energy to offer myself up as a teaching moment and run the risk of being harmed further. I am afraid of being told that I am not entitled to hurt or to be scared. I have been told that before, in word and deed, more times than I could count, and so in the moments of impact or even their aftermath, I am not in any kind of hurry to make myself more vulnerable by betraying my hurt.

Again, I am being belittled for my ways of difference. Again, she is trying to make up without apologizing. It is always again—being stared at, confronted, discarded, dismissed without being heard, stereotyped, taken for granted, or just plain treated poorly. And again, I am expected to swallow whatever the pain of it is. The injury may be someone else's fault, but it is mine to live with; nearly every time, the fault it creates in me is another place of weakness in a life that needs every scrap of strength I have.

I'm the tough guy, the big dog, I'm the one who can take it. No one need trouble themselves with an apology on my behalf. Don't worry about me. I will adapt, just like I always have.

I try not to cover it with anger. Sometimes I manage. But I understand those brothers of mine who lash out bitterly at anyone who tries to get too close to them. I mostly know better than to rinse it away with alcohol, too, but again, how else can we live with so much injury? I forgive them and thank G-d it isn't me. Even still, though, there's nothing to keep that injury at bay; it cuts close to the bone and stays there, solidifying every day it does.

There is only this sedimentary stone, the one that lies somewhere between my throat and my cunt, layers and layers of injury done to me without forgiveness ever being sought. Created by accretion, Hell's little pearl, heavy in my body. Weighing down my tongue so that it cannot make the shape of "I love you," rolling itself across my heart and keeping kindness at bay, sealing my body irrevocably against intrusion no matter what pleasure it may bring. And because I cannot deny or dismiss anyone, no matter how hurtful they are to me, because I do not want them to bear the kind of pain I have, I am doomed to accumulate further injuries, further layers of this stone, until I am dead and the matter is less pressing to me.

This is no way to live, but it's the only way I know. You, too. I love you for that, and for the way you encourage me not to take such harms into myself at the precise moment in which you are doing just that. I would urge you that you are more worthwhile, more deserving than that, too precious to lay yourself in harm's way. We try to protect each other, in our imperfect ways, and when we can't, we can at least stand and honor each others' hearts for their honorable stupidity. We do that, because there's nothing much else we can do. We look each other in the eye. We nod. We hold each other close, tenderly, usually when no one is looking. We saddle up and we do it again. Me, and you, and all of us, and all of our stones. We build walls, but we should make soup instead.

BUTCH IN THE STREETS, FEMME IN THE SHUL?

I have certain ideas about the treatment of others, the proper way in which to do things, the ordering of the world. In my daily life, I walk on the outside of the sidewalk and encourage the girls to order first. I stand to shake hands and hold doors open until everyone I can reasonably wait for, of whatever gender, has passed through. I do these things naturally, they feel like my tiny chance at grace, and it makes my heart and several other blood-rich organs swell when my wife smiles happily at me for opening her car door, or when a butch in the subway sees me give my seat away and meets my eye and nods. I interact with the public world like a gentleman. I help people get their bags down from the overhead compartment, and I let others go first, and I assume that what's left is fine for me, which it almost always is, and this all works very nicely and makes little old ladies who understand my gender, if not my genitals, pat me in a loving fashion and exclaim that the world needs more young gentlemen like me.

Things get exciting, however, when I am with my family.

They're not problematic about me being a butch; they seem to understand it and accept me and my femme wife and my studly ... er, manly ways with relative equanimity. But the men in my family, role models and gentlemen all, still think of me as female and therefore, by extension, a member of that class known as ladies when gentlemen are present. Even as the butch danger alarm sounds loudly in my head, even as each of my individual nerve endings starts to twitch and burn, I bite down and order my dinner with the women. I sit in my seat as though I were actually, literally glued to it and clutch it hard when a man comes over to shake my hand in order to avoid popping up like a jack-in-the-box and breaking his nose as he very properly leans in to be introduced. I twist and sigh and very reluctantly let a waiter pull out my chair for me.

I go to synagogue with my family, the whole great messy extended clan of grandparents and cousins and all, and my grandfather who is now five inches shorter than I am and a hundred pounds lighter and also-by-the-way-eighty-five-years-old reaches out when we get to the part of the path that isn't paved and takes my hand and puts it in the crook of his elbow to steady me as we walk. When I sit, I don't plant my feet, knees spread wide, and rest my forearms on my thighs during casual conversation; I don't use the booming voice of my butch lungs that can get the attention of a crowded room in full voice, but the musical one, a full octave higher, that I use to speak into silence when I give a speech.

Our rabbi, who has known me since I was the universe's most awkward preteen girl, puts a big, warm hand on the small of my back as we walk, guiding me with him. I try to make it look natural, but I know that if there's a butch watching ze's laughing hir ass off inside, seeing me suddenly trying to do the entire dance backward and in heels. Okay, not really heels. You know what I mean. But it does feel exactly like when I dance with my father or grandfathers, the only people left in the world who still want to lead me, and I have to hang on to my dad for dear life because he's the only lead I know stronger than me and can get me through. Paradoxically it's much easier for me to follow him, strong and sure as he is, and let myself be easy in his embrace than it is for me when I dance with my grandfathers, and their weak leads leave me helpless and ungainly on the floor. Without any traction I can't find a gender, or even a rhythm.

And then we go home, my wife and I. Invariably, after a day or two with my family I don't offer her my arm to take when we walk. I begin to forget to open her door for her when we go down to the car. When we get home it takes a whole day before I have my butch sense back, the one that shows anyone who needs or wants to or might enjoy some chivalry light up like a Roman candle in my inner eyes; it's a whole day before my body re-re-members what my brain knows and my heart never forgot: how to take my space in the world, bright anew. I used to think my butch identity was getting rinsed away in these encounters until I started to see it like a willow tree, responding to being cut back by flourishing.

AN APOLOGY TO MY MOTHER

Dear Mom,

There are a few things I've been meaning to say for some time now, things that you and I have never discussed, and before it goes any further, I have some things I would like to apologize to you for.

I'm sorry we never got to giggle about boys. I know you were pretty and popular, and that all the boys in the county wanted to take you out when you were a girl, and I know you really were looking forward to talking about dates with me, helping me choose the right top or the right earrings or the right boy for whichever dance, like you got to do.

You would have been good at it, I'm sure, good at all the parts, the talking about boys and sex and curfews and how to tell if a boy liked me and all of those key mother-daughter things. But I didn't really *like* boys, and I was too afraid to tell you until it was too late to see whether those skills could have reasonably translated themselves into the world of dating girls, too.

I never told you about my very first date, which I had with a redheaded girl from California who, after one date with me and one very chaste kiss, went back to her boyfriend in Davis and, as far as I know, is straight to this day. I never told you about my first time, which was extraordinary, with a beautiful girl on a cold and sunny fall afternoon in her bed at her boarding school when I was seventeen, when we got to take all day and all night and into the next morning; I never told you that it was better than I could have imagined, languorous and delicious and warm under all of her covers, wrapped up together all night. I might not have told you if it was with a boy, either, but I think you would have liked to have known, before now, that my first time having sex was safe and honest and everything else you might have hoped for, with a girl I loved very much.

I'm sorry about the shopping. I really am. I know you like it, and I know you had high hopes about long shopping trips for pretty things that we would casually lie about the cost of to Dad, punctuated with little lunches at which we would talk about all kinds of things. I'm sorry shopping was always such an ordeal because I hated everything you liked and almost all of what I fit into, and we always ended up fighting and one of us crying until the miraculous method known as the Lands' End catalog appeared on the scene, but that didn't really have the same sense of bonding, did it?

When I was eighteen I thought that going shopping with you to look at girly things was cause for all-out war, and now nearly thirty, I think, *Eh. How could it hurt? I don't have to buy it.* I wish I had humored you a little for all the ways you humored me; I wish I had bent a little bit for as much as you flexed to meet me. The conceits of the young, I guess. But separating seemed so important. I hope you understand, I was never trying to reject what you liked by saying it wasn't good or useful, by making it seem silly or by condescending to it. It just wasn't for me. At the time, it seemed so urgent, so vital, to make sure that I shoved femininity away from me as hard as I could, to protect myself from everything that seemed to come with it, everything I didn't feel comfortable with and still don't. It took the intervening decade and more to see that really, I could have just said, "No, thank you."

And I'm sorry that now I'm so afraid of what you'll think that I don't take you with me when I go shopping for the things that make me feel good and look good: my peculiar blend of clothes, so masculine but hardly ever manly, with my brightly colored shirts and ties. I wish I felt sure that when I came out of the dressing room, confident and sharp, you'd look at me with pleasure instead of faint shame, that this is your *daughter*, here, in the necktie. But I don't feel sure. So I don't give you the chance.

I'm very sorry about the big wedding. I know what you imagined: the bridesmaids and the shower and the giggling and my great-grandmother's pearl earrings and lots of people and choosing a wedding dress and shopping for a perfect mother-of-the-bride outfit and picking out china and all of the other business that comes with the wedding process. I keep thinking that maybe we could have made it a little bit more like that, if we'd tried a little harder, instead of the small, perfect, but ultimately frill-free wedding we chose.

All the girl time you didn't get, all the sharing and long brunches and mother-daughter bonding and clashing, all the borrowing of clothes and whatever else is supposed to come with it that you didn't get, I really regret. I feel like my gender cheated you out of something you would have enjoyed enormously, through absolutely no fault of your own.

I know this is late, and there's probably more that I can't think of now. I'm sorry for every time I accused you of not loving me for trying to do what you thought was best. I'm sorry I didn't give you better help in understanding what I was doing and what I was going through, so you could actually judge what might be best. I got afraid of all the parts of it, all the things I thought you couldn't handle or understand, and I decided the best way to keep things civil between us was to hide most of my life and just interact with you on neutral topics. I succeeded in keeping things civil, all right, but I prevented us from getting closer, connecting on a deeper level, because I didn't trust you to walk with me where I was going. I can't tell you how sorry I am for that.

I love you very much, Mom. I hope you can accept my apologies, and that perhaps we can go forward from here, and see what kind of friendship we could have.

Love always,

Me

PRINCESS PICKLE

My grandfather calls me by a set of pet names all his own: sometimes Hotshot, sometimes Pickle, sometimes Princess, and sometimes, on rare occasions of closeness, Princess Pickle. I'm an old-school archetype, a butch. Not one of the willowy blonde explicitly gendered lesbians you might see on prime-time or in a touchy-feely photo essay about the glorious diversity of a family unit, but a tall, short-haired bull in jeans and boots and a T-shirt with the sleeves hacked off. People call me Scooter or Buddy or even Sir, if they're not paying attention (or maybe if they really are), but not princess. Certainly not Princess Pickle. I am the person my friends call when there are heavy things to be moved or problematic exes to discourage, but I also love having someone in my life to whom I am still a princess, as fiercely as I love my grandpa.

Joanna Straight, my family's neighbor and dear friend for rising twenty years now, calls me Sha-Sha, a derivation of my first name, Sharon, which she arrived at after calling me Sha for a few years, and—as far as I can tell—eventually deciding that wasn't a cutesy enough name. This despite the fact that just hearing her call me Sha made me twitch a little bit. Even now, with the name Bear stitched all over my life and my great hulking self in physical evidence right in front of her, when she sees me she opens her arms wide, and:

"Sha-Sha."

In a voice that one could creditably use to address a conference. She is completely impervious to my gendered cues, not because she's clueless, but because she simply doesn't care. She knows how she prefers to express her affection for me, and it is bigger than my gender. After our wedding, a number of my friends considered trying to call me that, which I promptly discouraged but then also asked them, how many people they knew when they were twelve still liked them. So, you know, there are tradeoffs.

Sometimes I'll play the voicemail on the speakerphone when we have guests, because I'm doing too many things at once, and there's my grandpa, "Hey, there, Princess, it's the old man," and my grandma in the background "Hi, sweetie! Hi, Nicole!" and someone turns around and says snarkily, "Princess?"

And what I think is: thank G-d for the people in my life who can hold these two visions of me at once, and what I say is: "You're just jealous," which is almost always true.

Perhaps the person to whom you have offered your handkerchief will insist upon washing it and returning it. Don't be offended. This is very often an excuse to see you again. Accept gracefully and offer a way to be contacted. It is not surprising that ze might like to see you again when no one is crying or bleeding, when ze can enjoy the acquaintance of such a gentleman under nicer circumstances.

WHEN I CAN'T FIX IT

What I really would prefer is to be able to fix all of the problems of everyone I like even a little bit, including people I have just met but who seem pleasant or interesting. I would settle for being able to fix all of the problems of the people I love. I have a whole set of problem-solving behaviors and I am anxious to use them, in much the same way that I would stand up on the train to give my seat to someone who seems to need it more than I do: here is something I can address, and I do, and all is well. I may not be able to fix my fellow passenger's infirmity, but at least I can ease hir moment on the train. Sometimes the help required is more then I can manage, however, and sometimes it isn't for me to give. This is not my favorite thing.

This is more frequently the case with femmes, who will let me solve small problems. I can rescreen the porch, carry the boxes up to the attic, drive someplace, pick something up, drop something else off. On a good day. But I am not practiced at listening empathetically and then doing nothing. Just being there, they tell me, is something, just knowing that I'll be there again is something else, much greater, but in my one-note butch brain I am screaming for a problem that can be solved in thirty minutes or a phone call to the right person or a trip to Home Depot. And when I say, well, then call me when it gets bad, at least do that, they say that they will and don't, and when I ask why, this is what I hear: "Well, I knew I could, and that really helped me."

Which makes me glad, it really does, it just doesn't feel much like help. It just does not seem like enough to do, especially since

I am never really sure whether I have helped, or whether, in the inimitable, glorious manner of femmes, the girl in question is taking care of me even in that moment by making me feel helpful, even when I am trying like hell to take care of her.

The part of my heart that wants to lighten the load of my entire community, individually and collectively, one ounce at a time if necessary, frets and sighs over this. Not being able to fix it is the worst feeling I know, and it is also a thing that I was only just recently able to start talking about with the butches I know. It used to be we didn't talk about it because there was nothing to be done to fix it.

Now to engage in a stereotype: Butch problem-solving is quite often much easier. When the fellas have problems, we can talk about them and take them apart and put them back together into solutions. Lists can be made, plans can be formed, appropriate telephone numbers can be tracked down, experts consulted, timelines established, and progress made. It is the Admiral Farragut School of Problem-Solving method of friendship, and it's what I'm good at, and with butches and boys it's just the thing: a problem occurs when something is not yet solved, and we solve it, or at least we understand it and can plan some steps to solve it, and everyone feels better and then we can go and spit or scratch something. Very efficient.

Right, sure.

These are the problems, of course, that butches will confess to. These are the problems that butches—taught early and often to guard our secrets and especially our weaknesses lest they be used against us—will sometimes, after much prompting, admit exist. The most intimate kinds of problems, the ones which are fully as complicated as the problems of any other gender, and probably often quite similar to the problems of any other gender, get hidden. In being hidden, they become occluded, sclerotic—choose your medical terminology. They harden and deepen; they begin to block things and take them over.

We do not confess them for reasons that, I am sure, vary from butch to butch, but often because we do not want to be seen as weak, or as wanting. Because we are afraid that if we are indulging—because that, so often, is how it feels: like a luxury rather than a necessity—in solving our own problems then we will not have the attention or energy it requires to solve the problems of someone we love. Because we are afraid, terribly, paralyzingly afraid, that having emotional needs makes us somehow less butch, or that maybe it doesn't but it will nonetheless make us appear less in some other way—that it will speak to the lack we feel inside, the one that grows in us as soon as we see the first places where we are outside the standard deviation and refusing to be called in for dinner.

And so we turn our energy and attention outward. I turn mine outward, I look for ways to mend the world while ignoring what needs mending in my own heart; it is the shoemaker who goes about with holes in his shoes. Helping makes me feel like I am justifying my place in the world, the air I am using, and the blade of grass I am crushing with every step. If I am not really fully human, as has been suggested often in my life—if I am a thing, or an *it*—than at least I can be a useful thing. If I am hardening slowly from the root of my unmet needs and unexpressed fears, I want at least to be sturdy enough for children to climb on.

This becomes complicated and dangerous, however, when

there is really nothing to be done. Problems in real life, as much as I hate to admit it and rail against it constantly, are not usually solved with one phone call, one trip to the store. They are systemic, or they are so badly knotted up with other things that pulling on one end causes shifts all along the way, some of which are enormously undesirable by-products of the original good intention.

Some things simply cannot be fixed: loved ones cannot be made undead, lovers cannot be made trustworthy anew, and confidence cannot be bought by the three-pack at Costco. So when I come up against a problem I can't fix or help, I feel useless; I feel like I am not worth having around. I also get deeply afraid in the face of badness I can't soothe. I don't know how bad it will get, and I can't protect my loved one from the effects of it. It makes me *crazy*.

If I could, I would spend all of my time helping. I would loiter on street corners looking for people to help. You know butches, we're so action-verb oriented: What can I do? How can I help? And if there's nothing I can do, no way to open up the problem even a little bit, maybe let some air in there and maybe some light, then I feel like a failure. I feel as though I am useless, as though I have let down my side, deserted my post, abrogated my responsibility to the sacred butch trust of helping, mending, solving, making better, lightening the hearts or at least the loads of the people I love. I would rather suffer the indignity and violence of a thousand imbeciles who cannot parse my gender and must blame me for it than have to stand in front of someone I want to help with empty hands.

Because I am not a well person, because I am so conditioned

away from showing any kind of fear, sometimes my fear expresses itself as anger instead. I am walking with someone who had recently injured hir knee, and ze stumbles and falls. Do I ask, in a concerned fashion, if ze would like to rest a while? Do I gently express my worry, all the while underlining my care for my friend and my faith in hir understanding of hir own body?

Of course not. I start yelling like a nutcase, yelping "Jesus! What are we doing out walking around if it's that bad? Why didn't you tell me!?" What I mean, of course, is "I'm very worried about you re-injuring yourself, and I am enormously frustrated that I cannot make you all better with just the power of my love for you. I wish I could keep you safe always, and it is terrifying to me that I cannot even keep you from falling to the ground when you are a foot away. Please be very careful, you are so precious to me that it is terrible to see you hurt at all, ever, and I could never stand to lose you."

But of course, I cannot say that, not in the moment, no matter how good my intentions are. I mean to, I want to, I try. But in the end, I am always left later that afternoon sending an apology via email, lambasting myself for my terrible behavior, and wishing the god of such things would please very kindly turn up and fiddle with the wiring in here so I could please stop yelling at the people I love right when they're having a hard time. But really, though, I am just hoping to help. That is the intention I am full of, even when I screw it up in five directions at once.

BEING A DELIGHT

She says to me, one morning, "You're a delight to femme things," while we're talking about something entirely different. It sticks with me, because I'm starting to understand, maybe just that week, how many different kinds of femmes there are. I've been thinking about butch and femme as adjectives, kinds of women, kinds of dykes, but now I'm seeing butch as a whole gender all its own and femme too, and suddenly femmes are everywhere. I'm not yet noticing the XY-persons whose gender is butch as much, because I've been largely oblivious to the subtle ways in which masculinity and butchness are different, though a few fellows are starting to stand out to my newly awake eyes, but the femmes? Everywhere.

I walk around in the world as a butch, and I speak and act and think and respond this way, and the straight women and young girls and fags and other femme souls I encounter, the ones whom I always thought were the wives of big, dopey, accommodating, delighted husbands like me, I now recognize as the femme wives of butch husbands. And these wives, they recognize me as a butch just like the ones they have at home, plus or minus a few parts, and smack me around and tease me right along with my wife while I stand around and look befuddled but good-natured about it. They rumple my hair and laugh at my performances of good-natured helplessness and call me darlin' in just that way, and I see this whole new thing for the first time.

When I meet the husbands, they're not butches. They're men, staid and stolid or inflexible and unobservant, wholly without whimsy, as mired in man-ness as men can be, and their femme wives flirt with me extravagantly but in a way that these men don't read as flirting because, after all, I'm just a girl, right? Even as I hold out their chairs and my own wife's, wait until they pick up their forks to start eating, incline my head toward them while they speak, make silly jokes to see them laugh. Even as the women grasp my forearms (strong and resting on the table), smack my shoulders (broad, jutting slightly into their space), rumple my hair (short, tousled, and resolutely product-free).

Or I don't meet the husbands, and I still know them in a minute by the way their wives discuss them: "Oh, I could never get mine to do that," they say to my wife. They say, "Wow, you've got yours *trained*, huh?" while I am up and running an errand for my girl, or while I am exercising a little of my charm on them, giving compliments, making myself useful. Especially if I sense that these femmes are not getting the butch attention they desire at home, from their partners or a complicit friend, I fall into it reflexively: as soon as an honest-to-goodness femme appears my courtliest femme-aware butch behaviors swim right to the surface.

A certain kind of femme, one who owns her power as a femme and uses it to take me for a test drive a little bit, she puts me into butch hyperdrive. Suddenly, viscerally, I want to bring out every gentlemanly butch behavior I have at my disposal, plus shine my shoes. My butch desire to fix thing gets out and meets up with my butch desire to be a butch for a femme who likes butches, and I sit up straight and try to be a delight.

I love to be a delight, love to take my part in the timeless passion play of butch/femme, love the frisson of joy that comes when

I recognize my foil out in the world, when I hadn't been looking, or even when I had. I love to show my colors as much as a magician loves the gasps of an audience when the dove disappears. I love to lavish upon femmes an attention that is an entirely different thing than intention, though I also love to offer both and see what happens, which is how I met my wife, but that's another story. I love to watch them preen under it and unfurl their femme charms for me. They honor me so sweetly with their trust, and I try to honor them, each and all, as best I can.

This business of putting a butch through hir paces does not seem, by the way, to be a learned behavior, but rather an instinctive one; little four- and six-year-old femme girls that I meet in airports and ice cream lines regularly assume their command of me, asking me questions, telling me what they want and need. In their ways, they're looking for the right kind of audience, looking to have the right kind of attention; a kind of attention I can hardly describe, but one which I recognize as the sort that butches have for femmes. It is an attention heavy with some measure of restraint, a way of relating that is queered, with irony—here's the tough guy, the dude, the butch with the flashy moves and the nice manners, the man of things, and yet this butch, if he's a gentleman, and I am, doesn't make a move without the femme's intention being explicit and assured.

After the femme's interest and intention are sure, a butch may be more aggressive, may even be very aggressive, may fling her over hir shoulder and carry her off to the woods or the backseat or wherever. But what distinguishes a butch from a man right here is that the butch knows the differences between flirting and for-real; butches are femmes' break from the world of policing their sexuality, their sensuality. Femmes can be as hot as they want around butches; dress up, tease, play, perform as much sensuality or sexuality as they like and never worry (or should never have to) that they'll end up in a situation they didn't want.

And these femme little girls, already alert to the world of gender long before they have the words to explain it, understand in some animal way the dangers of men but come and stand right next to me. They pat my face and head like I was their old Lab, show me their toys, ask me question after question about science and history and books with total and unassuming trust that they are in no danger at all from me. It soothes me in a way I also have no words to explain when any delicate creature recognizes me as a safe place and comes to take a little rest on my lee side, or offers me the trust of behaving as though I am what I most want to be. I feel seen, in those moments; I feel relieved that there are people who can look at my tough-guy exterior and see that it is entirely created in order to be able to curl myself around my loved ones in times of danger or need.

CHAT, OR HOW I LEARNED TO FLIRT, PART 1

MsG: Don't apologize.
BearSir: Sorry ...
BearSir: ::ducking::
MsG: ::thwap::
BearSir: ::backing away slowly::
BearSir: ::sticking out my tongue::
MsG: Sticking out your tongue? Hey now, don't threaten me with a good time ...
BearSir: ::letting my eyes narrow slightly, smiling:: Any day, baby. Any day.
MsG: Oooh ...
BearSir: ::leaning a little closer::
BearSir: ::fixing your eyes with mine::
BearSir: ::running my hand through my hair::
BearSir: ::letting one eyebrow creep up slightly:: And I mean that.
MsG: ::breath catching in throat::
BearSir: ::reaching out one finger, running it slowly from your collarbone up your throat to your chin::
BearSir: ::tipping your chin up to me::
BearSir: ::leaning in closer::
BearSir: ::lips nearly touching::
BearSir: ::softly, full of breath:: Anytime.
MsG: ::melt::
MsG: Oh you ...
BearSir: ::big smile::
BearSir: ::tilting my head:: You, too.

MsG: Maybe I'll have to pack that red dress of mine if I end up in Mass ... The heels don't have straps, though. The dress does ...

BearSir: ::reaching into my pocket, fingering my knife:: Oh, not for long ...

BearSir: ::seeing it in a puddle on the floor::

MsG: (Don'tcha know it)

BearSir: Well. ::ducking, looking impishly up at you:: I meant the dress ...

MsG: But of course you did ...

BearSir: But all things can be arranged ::running my hand through my hair again, smiling at you::

MsG: (My, but it is hot in here, isn't it?)

BearSir: ::taking off my jacket:: It is, isn't it?

BearSir: ::rolling up a sleeve::

BearSir: ::dipping into the ice bucket, taking out a piece of ice::

MsG: Eeep!

BearSir: ::tracing it slowly across the back of your hand::

BearSir: ::sliding it up your arm, gently, carefully::

BearSir: ::pressing it into the hollow above your collarbone::

BearSir: ::opening my mouth, releasing my pink tongue::

BearSir: ::slipping the piece of ice into my mouth::

MsG: (3,000 miles away, and yer able to send a shiver up my spine ...)

BearSir: ::looking down for a moment, then back up at you::

BearSir: Feeling cooler, now?

MsG: Um ...

MsG: Perhaps in one sense, yes ... ;-)

BearSir: Well. Good then.

MsG: ::catching breath::

BearSir: ::smiling gently::

YOUR FAITHFUL SERVANT

Let me take that for you. No, kiddo, you don't have to carry any-thing, you go right ahead and I'll just make a couple of trips. Get in the house where it's warm. It's not that heavy. I can get it. This is dirty, you don't want to touch it. I'll wrestle with it, if you could just get me a towel? Let me drop you off, it's raining pretty hard. I'll go get the car. It's not that cold. Sure, I can help you. Three flights of stairs isn't that much. You don't have to take the shuttle, I'll pick you up. Four a.m. isn't that early. It'll give me a good start on the rest of the day. It'll be nice to have your company. Let me drive. You worked all day. I'll get this check. No, no, you can get the next one. Did I say that last time? You can leave the tip, how about that. Just tell me what you want to do whenever you decide. Last minute is okay. See if any of the other things you'd rather do work out, and if not it'll be nice to see you. I don't mind; I want you to have what you want. Don't worry about that, I'll take care of it. Let me make a few calls for you. Hold on, I have the number right here. Did you want me to go with you? I'd be happy to; it's no trouble at all. Sure, I have time. I always have time for you. Here's an extra twenty bucks. Pay me back when you can. I don't want you driving around with no cash at all. Are you cold? Take my coat. No, it's not bad out. Here, I have an extra sweatshirt in the car. Go ahead and take the last of it. I'm not that hungry to-day. Call me any time, day or night. I just want you to understand that I'm here for whatever you need. Yup, I can give you direc-tions. Sure, I have stamps. No, baby, that was great, just let me hold you now. Let me run out, it'll just take a second. I'll be back before you know it, and then you won't have to wait until morning. Sure, I'll look at it right now. It's no trouble. Sure, I can wait. Just let me know when you're ready, we can go. Sure, I'll come over and bring my tools. I don't mind. Sure, I have time. I always have time for you. Sure, whatever you need. Whatever you need.

Me? I'm all set. Thanks, though.

Don't make a big show of the presentation—no flourishes, no milady, no preening. You have already spoken volumes about yourself with your ability to produce this item; you are already the only one with any better defense against grief or exsanguination than a crumpled receipt. Take it out and offer it quietly, folded, below her sightline. If there are people around, turn slightly away as you do it.

THE DRAWBRIDGE

I don't always know when to let down my defenses. Then again, sometimes, I do—and I can't. The survival skill that kept me safe turns into a barrier that keeps me separate, and I cannot let it come down.

Sometimes we're talking, and you're spilling out all of your tenderest secrets like treasure, making yourself naked so that you can be understood because you feel safe with me, because you know I would never betray you. And when you're finished, when the moment comes for me to respond in kind, I am too afraid. Maybe I tell you something, something that makes you think I've let you in but is only the facts, and not the truth.

More likely I stay silent. I leave you alone in your confessions. I tell myself I'm doing it because I want you to feel heard, to feel like this is not misery poker we're playing, but in my heart I know that the truth is that I am stopped by my own fear of being seen. It feels so dangerous. Sometimes you never notice, but when you do you feel shamed by your sharing and it twists me up inside, but I'm helpless. I can't go any further.

Sometimes we're in bed, naked and warm after I have tried my best to give you all the pleasure I can make between my hands, lying quiet and close, and then your hand is on my thigh. You have let me into your body, shown me the rich and beautiful shape of your desire, and you want to offer me the same, but I cannot accept. The chorus in my head that says that no one would really want to touch me, that you are just doing it out of politeness, is so loud that I cannot hear anything else; not my own want, never mind yours. I flinch away without meaning to. I try to explain, or distract you, but I see on your face the sharp ache of rejection and I am powerless to heal it, even though it is not you I am rejecting. My own demons are raging in my body, barbed and bloodthirsty, and you are still the one reaching out to me in this moment and I am pushing your hand away. I can't go any further.

Sometimes you ask me what I want, what I need, knowing from the look on my face and the shadow behind my eyes that there is something I want so badly. You ask with your gentlest voice, but I continue to lie, continue to deny you; I don't know how to do this. I am afraid of being a burden to you, a nuisance and a bother, I am afraid that if I ask anything of you I will become more work than I am worth.

I don't want to be any work to you, just shade and shelter and fruit and fuel without any watering or pruning or feeding required. You know that's ridiculous, and you tell me so; you remind me that you have never denied me anything I have asked for. You remind me that I have encouraged you a thousand times to tell me the same things, to let me offer you what you need if you'll only tell me what it is. You're right, I have, but that seems like my job, not yours. I don't feel like I am worth the consideration, but you only know it as me refusing you the same trust you have offered to me, and it makes you so sad. But I can't go any further.

Please understand that I want to. Please understand that I wish I could, in all those moments, please understand that I have never, not one of the times, meant to hurt you. I know I have, and it tears me up inside, and I try to make amends later, but I know the damage is done in the moment. The moment in which

I cannot let that drawbridge down, cannot let you come across the moat and into the center of me, so often under siege. The apparatus is rusty from disuse, and I keep meaning to scour it down and oil it, but then I wonder if that's really a good idea, if I should really be doing things that make me more vulnerable.

I'm trying, I promise. I am learning, I promise. And I know that I have no right in the world to ask you to be patient with me; more patient, since you have already been so kind and I have hurt you so badly in payment for your kindness. But this turns out to be the price of loving me, the toll that my butch self takes on anyone I allow close: a tax of being turned away at the exact moment that you want more than anything else to be let in. I know it isn't fair of me to ask, that it's just like asking you to keep sticking your hand in the fire against the possibility that one day, it will miraculously not burn you. The truth is, I need you more than I can ever show. The truth is, I wouldn't blame you a bit if you turned away.

But don't. Please, don't.

DANCING

She and I both know the steps to this dance. But like a merengue or any of the more emphatic Latin dances, it has a beginning vocabulary and then an infinite number of variations, or ways to personalize, sometimes measured in speed, sometimes hand position, sometimes calculated incrementally in infinitesimal degrees of light between partners. I know this every time I meet a femme, every time I make that particular kind of eye contact, and I wonder what she expects of me, what kind of openhipped twist she's used to putting into her spins, whether she'll understand a certain kind of pressure on the small of her back as my signal to come in and be dipped, or whether it will make her want to turn again. So much depends, you see, on the previous instructors and partners. Once muscle memory kicks in, those old habits are very hard to break.

So I make an effort then, when I talk about the forms of butch/femme, when I want to speak or write about the mode, to stick to the basics. Gentlemen, open your arms, hold your elbows high, invite the lady into your embrace just so, welcome her but do not grasp her or collect her, merely make a space for her in your dance. Once you have a partner, take a small step forward to make sure you're both starting on the same foot, and then a small step back to confirm it. Now is the time to be sure your partner is ready to move with you, not later.

Begin with simple movements, an eight count, medium time, something to get your hips in sync, something to show you how much she wants to move with you, take a sixteen if you prefer, no rush. Now, signal and then send her out for a single turn, no hurry, a nice slow one, let her have the full eight count if she wants it, just keep the time with your feet and watch her turn, gentlemen, just watch her turn and then open your arms again and let her naturally return to her home spot, don't draw her in yet but don't stiff-arm her either; just keep your frame welcoming and she'll be right back.

Now. Another eight. Try it again. Get used to the height at which she likes to hold her arms, the set of her head, in case you want to look at her eyes, or brush her cheek with your breath, see how she likes to set her leading foot, so that you might surprise her with a turn or dip for which she will be in the perfect position and which will make her feel graceful as a falling leaf, but do not do any of these things yet, just watch, just watch.

Patience is the key here, gentlemen. Do not get a reputation for moving to a close pose in the first five minutes because there will be times when you will not want to do that, and it doesn't do to give offense to one's partners, now, does it? Certainly not. You must leave yourself free to ask many girls to dance, to begin a dance over and over, to have several dances with many girls and treat each of them with a gentle courtesy and natural courtliness. You must allow room to ask the wallflowers to dance and return them unmolested, however much they might like to be, to dance with young girls and old women, to find yourself sought after as a partner for the style of your dance, not only for your designs on the ladies, or theirs on you. As a gentleman, especially in a day and age of so many cads and ruffians, it is your charge to make sure that every girl who wants to dance gets to dance at least one song, and so: these first dances with a new partner, they are basic, and cautious.

Of course, though, of course you are looking for a special partner, of course in all of these dances with young girls and old, shy and forward, lovely and plain, you are looking for the one who escalates with you into the more complex rhythms of the merengue at just the right pace, someone who looks at you carefully from under her eyelashes after the fifth or eighth turn of the evening and signals that she is ready for something a little more adventuresome. And for this you must be ready with the things that are more exciting. You must learn the variations and possibilities but, what's more, you must be alert to the ones she already knows, and ready to adapt to her at a moment's notice.

Do not try to force her into one turn when she is clearly going a different way, adjust yourself and match her, learn her learning before you teach yours, become a partner for her, not a janitor who pushes his partner around the room like a broom, not a boor at the dinner table who steers every subject around to the one about which he knows anything at all. This may mean being willing to ask her to show you what step or combination she is trying to execute, and even to ask her to teach it to you. You should do this with good humor and good grace. There will be partners, certainly not ladies, who may deride you for not knowing already, but I think it better to find this out earlier rather than later, yes?

And there she will be, eventually, after however many partners, after however many dance halls and any possible amount of time, she will melt into your arms sweetly as caramel, and you will keep her warm and pliable as long as you have her there. Do not forget, every time you go to the dance hall or a ball to ask many partners to dance, to keep your end of the bargain, to do honor to yourself and your woman, but also do not stint yourself the pleasure of many dances with the girl of your dreams: she will make you look good, and keep you warm.

GETTING FUCKED

Butches are not supposed to like to get fucked. We are not supposed to admit, with words or by deed, that there is any place in our sealed, concealed bodies, in our seamless identities, which could be penetrated. Once there's an opening, a breach in our defenses, who knows who or what might sniff it out and use it against us. Butches wear the pants and keep them on, butches use our hands and mouths and cocks to bring the lovers in our lives to great screaming heights of pleasure while we miraculously come—hard, satisfying orgasms—from the joy of this, and this is our entire sexual repertoire.

Butch sexuality is about focusing our attention outward, remaining composed and in control, serious and searching, calculating what twist or turn might bring the next scream, might wring the next increment of shuddering delight out of our lucky partners, who are naked and writhing and openmouthed on the bed, who are tearing up our sheets and loving us for it. Trashtalking daddies, gentleman callers, footballers and dandies and bulldaggers all. Butches are tops, end of story, all day and certainly all night. People called me after reading Minnie Bruce Pratt's *S/he* to say, this passage there, do you think that means Leslie lets Minnie Bruce touch hir? There, like that? Really? Huh. I guess Leslie Feinberg isn't the butch I thought, after all.

Bullshit.

We're butches no matter what we like to do in bed; butchness is not defined by who does what to whom in bed, in the backseat, over the coffee table, or anyplace else. We may do all of the above-named things; I certainly have come from giving a lover pleasure, but we do any number of other things, too, other acts both sacred and sexual, which is what it is any time a butch takes you into hir bed or follows you to yours. It's an expression of trust from someone who makes a fetish out of keeping people out and away, away for safety, hirs and yours.

Let there be no mistaking, no whispering about me when someone hears someone else say something, no backchannel phone conversations. I let my beloved touch me. I want her inside me. I beg her to, sometimes. I sprawl myself out on the bed and arch my back, I get up on my hands and knees. I like to get fucked. I *love* it.

I back up onto your dick, bracing myself against the headboard, using my arms and the strength of my big frame all in service of keeping still and solid so you can get all the way in, so your cock hits bottom just the way I like. Opening me up, making a space in me where there wasn't one before, making me sing a constant stream of praise for you acting out your desire, pouring it into me, fucking me hard even as I exhort you to fuck me harder, even as I slip into porn-star dialogue. Fuck me harder, give it to me, slam it in, I love it. And none of it seeming trite in the sweat of the moment.

I forget about how I must look, about how this sounds, about the weight of years of butchness on my brain, on my back, about whether or how I might be punished with this later when someone finds out what I've done, finds out how I like it, and taunts me with it, tells me all about the ways in which I am not real, not worthy to call myself a butch. But the goodness and the *oh, yes* of this and the fresh and strange feeling of letting someone focus on me for a moment outweigh the cold light of examination right now, here, with you. I can only focus on how good it feels right now, how good you are right now, fucking me just the way you know I like it: not stopping, not stopping until I come, hard and yelling and then collapsing on top of me, damp, out of breath, sticky, still ready for action, still full of love for me.

MAKING HER FEEL …

When I first meet you, I understand immediately that you have no idea how beautiful you are, and it makes me first a little sad and then very resolved, in a way that few things but a femme who doesn't understand her own wonders can. Not that any femme can ever really appreciate how glorious she is, but—there are stages of this. You are at a very beginning one, just starting to see your effect on others, just starting to catch sight of yourself in a mirror and like what you see instead of loathing it, just starting to feel wondrous instead of wretched. I am a student of femmes, you see. I know the signs.

The truth is, you fill me with desire. Not just sexual desire, though I am certainly not immune to your exquisite charms, but also a different kind of desire, one that I have no language for. What I want more than anything with you is to make you feel as precious, as desirable, as worthy of the attention of a gentleman as you are. Like a lady, assuming that the lady in question is not bound by her position; like the prettiest girl at the hop. Like a girl who wakes up and puts on lacy matching underwear because you just never know what might happen in a day.

A femme once told me that I had inspired her to buy lovely matching underthings, that she had never felt like she deserved them before she knew me, and that still ranks as one of the nicest compliments I have ever received. I want for you to feel delightful and yet still real, not idealized and not put on a pedestal but still capable of bringing a butch to hir knees with desire even though ze knows about your faults and foibles.

So, I focus the fullness of my gentleman butch gallantry on you. I watch you for moments of hesitation, and I pour myself into them so you can step gracefully over them in your cute shoes without fear. I remember what it's like to be seen, really seen, at first, how shocking it is to find someone who is looking at you and seeing something resembling the best mental picture you have of yourself, exhilarating and exhausting, and I keep the thrill of it on the tip of my fingers as I take your hand and settle it into the crook of my arm when I walk, as I gather up your hair or brush it back, as I find you a drink and a glass and settle you down at a table and keep my attention on you until you feel utterly diverting, completely entrancing, until you understand that I am helpless in your orbit, in the thrall of such an extraordinary femme, a girl of such beauty and grace.

In a way, this is an act: I am not helpless, not really. I could drag myself back if I had to, I could refocus my brain on the ordinary stuff of life and what's happening around me, I could resist the pull of your gravity. But what's important in this moment is that I don't care to. The truth is that I would rather sit and flatter you and ask you questions and listen to the answers with my head inclined toward yours so I don't miss a single word than do anything else, and so rather than being helpless I am making a conscious choice to let go of most everything that I carry around in my brain because you are a much brighter light, and I hope you understand that that's a pretty serious compliment.

I show you what a struggle it is to remain a gentleman in the face of such sensuality every time you brush your skin against mine or let me get a whiff of your perfume, reapply your lipstick, or fuss with your hair: I want you to know that you're enough to make a good dog break his leash, and that only my lifetime of practice in courtliness to femme things keeps me within the bounds of propriety, darlin'; that you'll always have me close to the edge but also that I'll never cross it.

Darlin'. That's one of the words I use in place of your name. I never know how any girl feels about her name, who has misused it before I get to it, and so I slide my voice down into a register of endearments and bring out my favorites: darlin', I call you, peaches, sweet pea. Sugar pop, sweet thing, beautiful girl, baby-cakes, rock star, dearheart, and sometimes just Baby. Like when you walk into a room and I see you for the first time, or when you look sad, and I need a word small and dense enough to carry all of my concern and love on its back, a little workhorse word.

Baby does the trick. It slides out of my mouth full of breath, my throat relaxed around it, wanting the least resistance between my affection and your understanding of it, and you hear every-thing that comes with it, and even if I don't call you by your name you understand that I am nonetheless naming you—naming you so precious, such a great treasure in a world of mundane things, and myself blessed to be allowed to sit in the sunlight of your smile for a little bit, to be allowed to put my gentlest hands on you and let you feel in them the warmth of my esteem and the heat of my desire.

BEING A SHOPPING SWITCH

We're going shopping.

When I go with her, I make sure I look presentable, like the kind of boy a girl wouldn't mind if the other women in the dressing rooms saw and knew was hers; I put on a clean button-down shirt and tuck it in, and comb my hair. That's how I spend a lot of my shopping time when I go with her, waiting outside the dressing room to either give my opinion or receive my instructions. I am given to understand that in the case of women who shop without their own personal shopping bottoms the salesclerks will happily get them the same shirt a size smaller or see if this comes in a darker blue. I see them perform these tasks for other shoppers. But like hospital wards, where there is not enough help for everyone who wants helping, bringing along your own fetch-and-carrier is the best bet if you don't want to wait. So I stand, or if I'm lucky and the management has provided husband chairs, I sit outside the dressing rooms and wait for my next assignment.

We go from store to store, trying things on and inspecting them. I give my opinions on dresses and shoes, blouses and lipstick colors. Sometimes I say things that make the other women look at me, agape, as though my mouth has been possessed by that flighty queen from *Queer Eye* even while the rest of my body still looks like any other big dumb boy's. I say that I like a skirt but I wish it were bias-cut instead of A-line, or that I am not fond of the fashion for surplice tops, or that the post-WWII idiom in shoes this season is amusing but rarely looks good on actual feet, or that I like the look of a bolero jacket. I know the names of colors, heliotrope and coral and Nile blue, and I can say without hesitation whether a lipstick might look better matte with a bit of powder.

These other women look at me with wonder, their boyfriends and husbands having made a fetish out of refusing to learn such words under any circumstances, as though merely pronouncing the word "periwinkle" or "princess seam" could easily turn a strong man gay as a box of birds. They say to her, "That's your husband?" in voices that loiter between admiring and disgusted, as though they know that there's no force on earth that could make their men or boys take such an interest in their clothing and they think they might really prefer that to the spectacle of me, filling an armchair, legs crossed ankle over knee, looking just right until I say "tea length."

I don't much care. They're not my job; she is. I get sent off to collect an example of everything in black, in a Capri length, in her size. That's my job. The salesclerks try to help me, but I won't really let them. I'll let them point me in the right direction, but when they try to take over my job and send me back to my chair, I refuse, politely. It's not that I fancy myself better at it; I'm sure it takes me twice as long and I nearly always miss something and also nearly always bring back something egregiously outside the parameters of my assigned search. But I am performing something here that is very important to her, and abrogating my tasks to someone else, however helpful, is not the point.

The point is that she wants other girls to see what it looks like to have a boy so crazy in love with you, as I am, that he will spend an afternoon talking about Capri pants, to have a boy so delighted by you that he never calls you by your name, but addresses you always as "beautiful girl," or "my love," or occasionally and with great fondness, "boss." To have a boy who will happily fetch your next-size-down and carry your bags and charm the salesclerks at the register without flirting overmuch and just generally try to make himself as useful as possible, all for the dizzy and undying pleasure of making you happy. And even though I am not a boy, I look like one, and so I can be complicit with her in this kind of wonderful afternoon, part indulgence of her great beauty and style, part guerilla feminist activism.

Later, when we walk through the mall or down the sidewalk, me laden with packages that are clearly hers, I watch the eyes of the people we pass: the women who look at me with a certain longing, wishing they had their own boys to carry the bags. The men who look at her with an unmistakable hunger, wishing that they had the honor of schlepping for a girl like her, and then look at me with a certain edge of disbelief, not quite clear about why I get to squire this marvelous example of femininity around when they are clearly wealthier, more handsome, better hung. I have learned to meet all of these gazes with a calm kind of sweetness. There's no point in defensiveness or sheepishness or challenge. I'm the one holding her bags.

When I go shopping with him, I also get a little shined up. I make sure my boots are polished and my sleeves rolled up just so. I march him into the store on a mission. It is time to deal with the clothing problem. There is always a clothing problem being dealt with on these trips, and it can only be handled by a radical wardrobe assault. I have already peered at everything in his closet, already taken note of sizes and styles and designers; I know which manufacturers cut their clothes for what kind of bodies. I have a plan, and a budget, I make straight for the racks that hold the first thing I am looking for while he trails behind me, looking slightly lost and slightly afraid.

I rip through the racks quickly, easily discarding anything that isn't a good color, a sturdy enough fabric, cut well, sufficiently masculine for him. He stands slightly behind me, trailing his fingers across the shoulders of the garments I have just been though like a mowed field until the pile of clothing I heap into his arms is so large that he needs both of his hands to manage it.

Intermittently I stop, deciding, and hold something up to consider it. He might say what he likes about it, or not, but I come to this assuming that if he knew much at all about how to dress himself I wouldn't be here in the first place. I examine and approve piles of jeans and chinos, stacks of button-down shirts, a handful of ties, a heap of underwear. Shoes pave the bottom of the shopping cart he eventually fetches, until I have exhausted the place of every single thing in his size I find acceptable, and we go off to the dressing room.

There is rarely a husband chair here; it is usually a large discount store with side-by-side men's and women's dressing areas, so I bully the fitting-room attendant into giving him a tag for the maximum number of items on the men's side and send him in with instructions on what to try on first. I wait outside with the occasional mother and the even more occasional girlfriend. Sometimes one of them will ask me, very tentatively, "Your son?" in a voice that suggests that if he isn't they really don't want to know.

Mostly I nod, wondering if they think I am his mother or his father, and wait for him to reappear, hair messy, shirt untucked, pants pooling around his ankles. I sigh, and kneel in front of him, daring him with a glance to make a lewd remark as I fold his cuffs under until they're the right length and tell him to tuck in his shirt, and where's his belt? He didn't get a belt. Fine, I say, appraise the outfit, tell him to keep the shirt and forget the pants, to put on the dark jeans and the black shirt next, and I'll go see about a belt.

Prowling the racks for the right belt takes a little while, but no one tries to help me or remarks on me while I'm doing it, and when I get back there he is, shirt tucked in, jeans cuffed up around his furry ankles. I hand him the belt and he threads it through wordlessly while I look at the clothes again, tell him I like the shirt, keep the jeans on and try the blue striped one. We go on like this for a while, pants and shorts in various combinations; he periodically brings out the no pile and I give him a fresh stack of things to be tried on while the fitting room attendant ignores us, not even trying to keep count, and he preens under the attention of coming out in better and better outfits, liking the look of himself in the mirror more and more as we zero in on the best colors, the nicest cuts for his body.

Young boys come and go with their mothers, reluctantly shrugging on shirts and wandering out indifferently in baggy jeans, grown men go in alone and come out the same way, holding a golf shirt or a pair of slacks as they make their way up to the counters to pay. He is the only thing blooming here on the silent men's side, the chatter of women and girls floating over occasionally in bits; he is standing up straight by now, tucking in every shirt, making a good try and tying the ties once in a while, parading out with a smile while I approve and dismiss clothes and combinations. Keeping a running tally of what's still in there with him is easy, so is the commentary as I look at the clothes, pointing out what I like about them for his next, possibly unaccompanied shopping trip. See how this one is structured, with a separate shoulder placket, I say, and show him the lines of stitching to look for, look at this box pleat, see how the pockets of these pants are set a little higher. He examines everything and nods solemnly.

When we're done, we make the final choices, according to my recommendation and his budget, talking about the utility of each item. You can wear this for work, I say, and to go out in. This tie goes with all three of these shirts. He pays, and I usually surprise him by springing for the one thing he loves but couldn't afford: the shirt that was perfect but too expensive, or the tie he really doesn't need but loved.

"Just a little present," I say, "a little starter gift to go with your new clothes."

The clerk ringing us out says "Isn't that nice?" while he blushes and hugs me, says thank you to my neck in a way so fond that suddenly no one thinks he's my son. We walk out and to the car, him holding the bulging shopping bags, and he gets in and pulls them onto his lap, fingering the fabrics and looking so pleased. I ask him, does he have plans tonight, somewhere he can wear what we've just picked out, someone he can surprise in them?

I always hope he does. I always want there to be someone he loves waiting, someone who thought he was handsome anyway, someone who will be delighted by the fresh shirt and tie he'll show up in. I hand him some collar stays, and show him how to put them in. I think about him walking down the street dressed up in his fine new clothes, the mercerized sheen of the fabric bound to fade but not the love he knows I have for him, shimmering faintly on the surface of the cloth only to his eye, something no number of washings can rinse away.

LAYING DOWN WITH A BUTCH

There is a kind of connection that I sometimes have, with certain people, a way of trust that only comes with people who have what I always think of as a butch heart. That's not quite right. Some of them don't identify as butches; some, in fact, hardly identify as anything even in the same zip code. But it's a very boy way of being bigger than, a sturdy and quiet way, taking care of everyone around you as best you can, always trying to fix it, always stepping up to do the crap job that gets no recognition, and also of being so gentle, so generous, so nonjudgmental of other people, believing that they are doing their best.

Is that sexist? I don't mean it to be. I mean to describe this way of some masculine things, so different in its energy from other ways of caretaking. In Yiddish, this is referred to as being a *mensch*, which also means a man. There's a part of me that wishes I could separate it entirely from gender, and another part which sees it as exactly right that this is gendered, that there are ways of butchness that are composed of the best of masculinity and leave all of its boorish excesses behind.

But I met this butch, a handsome writer with a toughness about him that I recognized as the result of his life for the forty-six years before he and I crossed paths, a toughness that even still showed an underlying playfulness. That he had been able to keep that place alive and tender in the hardness of life made him light up my eyes as someone who would know some of the things I knew, someone who would honor the same places in me, and we started talking. Talking turned into flirting, and flirting turned into intention. We made a date to spend an evening together seeing what our combined toughness and playfulness might mean when we took our clothes off, a kind of old-style faggot good time without a lot of expectation about who might or would do what, to or for whom.

That's rare for me. I usually come to new lovers with the expectation of topping, which I certainly love and find delightful, which feeds a part of my soul that knows about all of the ways to give love, some of which look nothing like what Hallmark suggests and are yet so full of care and good intention that there's no other word for them than love.

Well, except when I turn up and people are clearly expecting AutoTop, The Animatronic Dildo™, but that's another essay entirely. Anyway. I don't switch much, don't really want many people to fuck me, because there's a whole code, unwritten but no less rigid than if it were chiseled in stone, about how Tops Must Be, how Butches Must Be, and it does not include taking off one's pants. It does not include admitting to one's own desires, only quietly serving the desires of others. It certainly does not include taking a break once in a while to inhabit some other gender, role, or sensibility, even for half a delightful, sweaty hour, in the company of someone who feels like a mirror of me rather than a complementary piece I can fit myself against.

I can't do it, if that's the gaze that beholds me. I can't bend over for someone who sees it as even vaguely shameful that I want to, can't do any of those things with someone who sees it as incongruous for me to want to, can't get on my knees for someone who is thinking gleefully that ze has flipped me. I am not spending an entire lifetime trying to get comfortable in my own identity, in my own skin, only to offer the tenderest, most tentative parts to people who I might not be able to trust to hold them safely and return them unscathed.

On a rare occasion, though, very rare indeed, I meet someone like hir, someone who feels to me like I feel most days: tired, overworked, overstimulated, underappreciated, and still delighted with hir life and everyone in it, even the problems and the stresses. Someone who recognizes, as I do, that responsibility comes with work, that it comes with inconvenience, and who still is quietly delighted to serve those things about which ze cares, even when the individual actions are difficult or unpleasant or merely inconvenient. Who appreciates that being responsible for things is a good and precious thing, that it's what makes us the people we are, that those offices of trust are what separates us. Someone who appears shameless to the world because the shame voices in hir head are so accomplished that other people's attempts just seem crappy and amateur, like calling the fat kid Fatso, so easily ignored. Someone whose good nature has been taken advantage of for so long that ze is scared all the time, and yet is such an optimist that ze saddles up and keeps trying anyway. This is the guy-type-thing who is not just willing but *pleased* to give me a break from being the Big Dog for a little while. Ze is strong enough to hold everything I carry around with me for a few minutes so that I can put it down, and I can do the same for hir; when I do, ze is just as amazed as I sometimes am not to have to do all the work, for once.

We can't help but try to soothe each other, when we meet. It takes all kinds of forms, simple and so complex, but this one I'm talking about is the naked kind. It's such a reassuringly tangible thing, to keep the watch while someone who is constantly keeping tight control over hirself and everything around hir lets someone else hold it all for a minute and just lets go. We do it in a lot of other ways, try to ease each other, try to hold it all, but most of them are the talky ways that our butch hearts sometimes distrust, can't quite see as being real help; only a few are so stark against the weave of our experiences that they feel undeniably readable, incontrovertibly present and accounted for.

I love to be trusted in that way. I try very hard, in every intention and deed, in my private life and my public presentation, to be someone who *can* be trusted that way, someone safe, someone who people know will take good care of them. With them. I put my hands on people very gently, I listen to them as carefully as I can, I hold myself just firm enough to be a windbreak but not so rigidly that I can't change direction, and I hope that people will see it, will come and take some reprieve behind the trunk of me, or in my shade.

Lots of people trust me like that. I trust very few. I want to, so much that sometimes I trust when I know I shouldn't and I get hurt that way, but when I need to trust someone else with the load I'm carrying, I have to be careful that I choose someone who can handle it, who won't be bent to the ground by the sheer weight.

Last night, I found another one. And the feeling is so searingly sweet, so incredible, that I want, I really want to write about it. But I don't know how to explain. It's as organic and electric as lightning, yet seems so mundane, when I try to write it out, like every poem about lightning, so tawdry in its way. I can't get there, can't explain what it feels like: to get twenty minutes off, where I am usually keeping at least one eye and half of my energy on everyone else and whatever comes along. And I'm hardly ever safe, because the nature of people is that any time you let yourself be vulnerable it's a sign of weakness, and there's always someone looking at me to see how I am weak so they can bring me down, from inside the community or outside it. Even as I type that I imagine some people scornfully dismissing it as my own self-important paranoia, but you can see the scars perfectly well if you take a moment to look. To not worry about what I say, to not feel like each phrase, each construction is being rated against someone's internal Butch-O-Meter and may at any time be found wanting. To have the cold and inert load of judgment and expectation that I carry around with me every day like a sackful of anvils replaced by the warm, furry, expectant weight of a butch lying prone along the length of me, skin against skin, smiling playfully at me with a generous look in hir eye.

Instead, I try to describe the event: Ze fucked me.

That doesn't really cover it.

Then I try more, in the same vein, thinking in what I also think of as the classic butch way that if something doesn't work, well, just try harder. Hard is right, here: really hard, the way I like it, muttering filthy things into my ear and hauling me back onto hir dick by my hair and encouraging me in the hottest, sweetest way until I came, screaming, and ze then wrapped hirself around me and breathed into my hair until I calmed down, until I came back to myself.

But that just seems like crappy porn trying to dress up in good clothes. It doesn't do justice to the feeling that sparked palpably between us, ultraviolet in the eventual dark, filaments of a fragile trust between two people who don't trust well. Only by explaining how far I am from being able to bring words to the emotion can I even show the size and shape of it. I am as silent in the face of it as I have been at the mouth of the Grand Canyon; it is a thing too vast and too wondrous to put words to. Every attempt feels cheap and incomplete. I wave my hands at it, and then I turn half away and look off into the middle distance in what I think of as the classic butch way of signaling something of great importance.

Writing this is difficult all on its own; I'm aware with every keystroke that I'm making a record of something that should probably not be recorded, something too delicate to bear the weight of words, something too dangerous to leave a trail toward. I can't know in what ways this evidence might get used against me, in a way that the deed never will be, because that piece of time is guarded by another member of the tribe, someone who won't betray my trust, who will keep my secrets and never make me feel secretive about them, who will keep the same careful watch ze kept when I came unglued at the end, watching and judging every stroke, breath, eyeblink, heartbeat, making sure that everything was as it should be, keeping me not only in the moment but in *my* moment, leaving me free to feel.

I had this moment of being freed in my own body, in my own mind, and it felt like a gift, as much a gift as when I move a friend and bear the weight of his furniture so he doesn't have to. This butch bore the weight of my fears, of my heart, of my history for a moment so I didn't have to. I felt so light, in those moments, light enough to take flight. I feel so settled, today, like something in my always-busy brain, normally noisy and distracting, has been shocked into silence, or is perhaps sullen in defeat.

The truth can only be seen in the artifacts, and they are small enough to understand and assess on their own: I felt so safe that a few tears actually ran down my cheeks, and I never cry anymore. For me, this was a revolutionary thing—I was safe with hir. I felt it, for a long moment, like perfect balance on the trunk down across the stream; like the part of a dive that feels like soaring that comes just before the part that feels like falling. I knew it down to my bones, a kind of space opened up there where the muscles usually clutch against my skeleton and let me fall loose against hir for a little while.

TOUCH

I reach out and touch the people I love. I do it to soothe, to flirt, to make contact, to connect, to speak a thousand things for which our language has no words: my feeling of belonging to them, to this tribe; my great and inexpressible joy about my family of friends; the hope I have for our future, singly and collectively.

I do it because I was raised in a house that was full of touch, roughhousing and hugging, kisses goodnight and rumpled heads, and so hands—in my hands, on my head, tugging or poking or gently just resting on me—feel like home. And I do it because now I can. I lived, except at home, in a world of no touch for so very long, of no hand-holding friends in middle school, no sling-arms-around-shoulders high school buddies, no sweet kisses goodnight at the door, no locker-room grab-ass that now I seek touch as though I am making up for lost time. I lean into it as though all those missed years of lying in a big warm puppy pile of friends à la *Dawson's Creek* during my school days had an absolute value that I could achieve, surpass, if I work at it hard enough now.

I know what my hands and body are capable of, in the language of touch, what things I can say with them. I have learned to give a hug that makes the person I embrace feel like time has stopped, like all threat is at bay, and I have learned to drop my hand onto a child's head with exactly the right firmness to say "I claim you, and I love you, but I promise not to try to hold you here." I know how to kiss a girl's neck just so, with enough ardor to report the volumes of my esteem for her, her brilliance and her beauty, without making her feel as though anything more than the gracious acceptance of my affection is desired. I know how to lay a hand along a young man's cheek and make him feel approved of, as though he has been measured and not found wanting.

At the same time, I am aware of the power of my arms, my hands, even my jaws. I use them gently, deliberately, on my friends and family to remind myself constantly of their most correct uses; I use them to battle back against all the times, every day, when my fists clench with rage, arms tighten by my sides, jaws clamp down in disbelief at the way I and my beloved band of outlaws are seen, dealt with, treated, disregarded. I keep myself grounded in the right purpose of my limbs, my trunk, by using them as often as I can to give shade and shelter. I do this even when in my secret heart I am embodying the trees along the Yellow Brick Road, throwing apples and using my branches as spears, pinning miscreants to the ground and dripping sap onto them until they're stuck, stilled, fastened in the slime of their own shortsighted stupidity with me standing over them, laughing my woody laugh. But I have learned that I can become by doing, that making sure I reach out with a palmful of fondness every time I extend my hand allows me to meet people where they are.

Perhaps more than either of these, though, I touch to transgress. To be visible as a butch who is delighted by the feel of hands on my body, other bodies against mine, to show myself as a butch who relishes touch, who has finally come to a place where I am not stilled by gender or expectation, by disappointment in my body or fear of that in others, or shame. I reach out for my friends, my lovers, my family. I pull them close against my body which is and will always be topographically female, and has been so often shamed for that. I want for them to feel my actual body, my desire and my comfort, the heat of my skin with them close, and also—also I go on hoping that if I do this enough, if I can keep people who see my body as acceptable, or even attractive, next to it enough that their attitudes will seep through my layers, through my skin and under it. I keep hoping that one day I will look in the mirror and be pleased to see exactly what I see; I'll believe in the looks on my lovers' faces when I turn to them, naked, wanting. I think hard about everything I have to swallow in order to have pleasure in my life, and I see very clearly exactly where that line is drawn for me, what I am not willing to give up. I reach out and touch, and hope.

THIS GESTURE

Of all the ways in which I might touch someone, in public, wrapping my arms around hir from behind is the most fond, it is the one that communicates most specifically that I want someone to feel treasured, and also protected. I clasp and hug, I pat on the back and kiss cheeks, I have a whole vocabulary of ways of affection. We all do. This is the one I use when I am feeling as though someone does not understand as well as I would like how dear ze is to me, or how precious ze is to the world. I walk up behind you in a bar, a store, wherever as long as you already know I'm there, and I hold you briefly, sweetly.

It's not a careless gesture; I do it in steps and with calculation, wanting you to feel all the things I want you to feel, in the order in which I want you to feel them. It is full of fondness and ego, protectiveness and protectedness. Complicated in my brain in ways I imagine the body never could unpack or measure, like a movie explosion. You would have to go frame by frame to see every detail, to know exactly where the point of impact was and what ignited and how it spread. And why would you want to?

You see it: explosion. That's the sense of it, it's enough to carry the plot forward so you can see in what improbable contrivance the hero is protecting hirself from it. But at the creation end, where untold dozens of technical people and safety officers and G-d alone knows who all else are laboring, days or weeks or months go into the creation of the moment, and when they see someone else's explosion they know where the par cans were and how the corners of things were joined so they would fly apart just so and a thousand other tiny details. I want you to see that end of this gesture, want you to understand what I am doing exactly, so that you hear everything I am saying to you and how I am saying it.

First, I come to stand behind you. I'm leaning back on my heels; I take the last step and then more slowly bring my body into line behind yours. I want you to feel that there's someone behind you before there's touch; it says that I am not trying to sneak up and gives your unconscious time to start processing the information your rational brain can't even fathom: the scent of me, and the height and breadth of the slight heat of my body, the sound of my footfall and the items in my pockets, the speed of my breathing. All tiny things, and none of them alone would give you any real clues to who I am, but taken together they carry maybe enough information to soothe you that I am friend and not foe. Especially you, you who are so prickly and defensive in life. You all are, and it makes me sad, it makes me want to have been standing behind you for a lot longer, through the bad parts, and perhaps that intention held so palpably in my heart is part of why this movement delights you. I'm behind you, I am saying, and I am backing you up.

So I do that, and then I lean in, just a bit, letting my chest touch your back just a second before my hands light on your hips, showing you that I am not intending to grab but to hold. I don't know when I realized that the breadth of my chest against your back would mitigate the message of my hands touching your body, but it does. It is one of the things I learned working bar jobs; there is a way that a broad touch and open palm, a chest, the length of a forearm, is less startling and also has less offensive potential. So I am showing you my intention, and in this moment I am also protecting my vulnerable underside by pressing it against you. I do not think it goes unnoticed.

My fingertips come to rest first, firmly, no tickling, and also alert for stiffening. I don't want this to feel like an attack. I want it to feel like sinking into a comfortable chair, and if there's the hint of resistance my hands glance off and I take a step back so you can turn around and face me. Usually, that doesn't happen, usually you are already in the understanding of who is behind you on some level and my voice in your ear is just the confirmation for the officious wonks in the brain department of what your skin already knew.

But if it does feel like an attack I understand; there's no one of whom I am very fond who has had an easy time of it. We all have our damage, and if today is not a day in which you are pre- pared to be embraced by someone you cannot see with your eyes, I will never take it personally. I will kiss your cheeks warmly and hold my body just slightly away until you move forward enough to make contact with me. I know how it goes, sometimes. But if it isn't that day, if you are still or alerted-but-not-resistant to my hands then I will slide them along your waist until they are around you, until they meet in front of you and perhaps rest on your belly if I think you're having a good enough body day for that, or hold your belt buckle, or they curl around your hipbones or clasp each other. Still, I don't pull you in, I just make the circle, enclosing you in a useful motion of binding that restricts nothing.

At this moment, it is just a hug, a backward hug, but a hug nonetheless, and if it speaks to you about my willingness to look in the same direction in which you are looking and wrap my body around yours for warmth or safety, well, those are bonuses. Just like it's a bonus that you have told me, by now, that you know the feel of me well enough to recognize me behind you and trust me enough to have me where you cannot see me, touching you unsupervised. I am not sure I could say all of these things to you, but I can show them to you in this language of motion, in this little dance step which is not quite done.

Done is right here: I take a breath in when my hands meet, and then breath out and you lean into my exhale, giving just a bit of your weight to my frame, relaxing into my embrace. Maybe you put your hands over mine, or on my forearms, maybe you just keep talking, maybe you sigh. Sometimes, extravagantly, you lean your head back against my shoulder and half-close your eyes, speaking volumes of trust for such a watchful creature. But in whichever way, you complete the circuit of welcome, you offer your heat and protection to me just as I offered it to you. We're both a little safer for a minute or two.

YOU

I understand in some way, charmed and undefinable, that I was put on earth to soothe you, to smooth your way, to light your path. I don't always know what it is that I'm supposed to do, or how, but I look for it. I search every day for the next thing, and the next. This is why I always want to fix it for you, why I can't leave a need unmet if I know about it or even a desire, however frivolous, because it's a tiny piece of the big picture, and I don't want to leave any pieces out. I didn't meet you finally until so late, and there are so many years of lost time to make up for.

I want to amuse and delight you, to comfort and calm you, to challenge and excite you, and I live and die for your approval. So much so that I'm sometimes challenged to be your partner because I just want to be your valet, tireless and nearly silent, looking constantly for the next thing I might be able to do. The smile you give me when I correctly anticipate what you want, and do it right, sparks in my heart a delight unmatched in modern times. It makes all of the hard parts worth it, everything I had to fight through, or for, to be a butch, to be an unadulterated bulldagger in a world of Standard American Television Gender, is worth it to see how your face looks when I appear from the other room, ready to go out, shirt starched and tie straight and hair tamed and hands open to you. To see what it looks like when I open hands to you while we're dancing and you take them both in yours, so cool and gentle and making me so much yours, claiming me just like that.

I am a butch for you. It's my own identity, but the first time

I saw you, laughing at a table in that dark bar with those boys, I knew why I'd never given it up even in all that time, all that trial. I understood you as the nameless future that kept me focused and progressing even when no one outside my body, my brain, my heart could understand why on earth I didn't give up and go back, or put it down, or lay low a while. I knew that if I didn't burn every minute I wouldn't harden enough, wouldn't shine enough, and that you might not notice me when you saw me, or want me if you did, and there would be nothing after that. You make it all worthwhile, you loving me: stubborn in the face of society and family, strong for my loved ones and tender for you, makes every slur I ever ate, every door that ever shut on me, every heartbreak seem like nothing because I can delight you now, as a butch, your butch, the butch of your dreams.

And so I stand here in front of you, every day, seeing the love in your face and the look in your eyes, and there's nothing in the world that I could deny you. You could carve your initials in me like a tree, cut me open and drink my blood; I wouldn't dream of refusing, but I know that I can nourish you this way, by being exactly who I am in the world for you. By looking always for ways to make your life a little better, a little brighter, lighting your way a little more, giving you whatever you will accept from me for as long as you will accept it, which I hope will be a lifetime. Because without you, my butch life, my queer life, my strange and curved life has its hope, its triumphs, and its pleasures, but no home.

Whatever happens in any individual interaction, with any individual handkerchief, remember this: remember that you are making a space for everyone who encounters you in these moments to feel as though there is kindness in the world for them; that there are people who can look beyond their own needs sometimes, and see the needs of others. It is that quality in you that makes me tell you all this. Make sure you don't ignore your own needs, that way lies loneliness and disappointment. But keep your eyes open for others, and ease their discomfort as best you can. Use whatever you can spare.

Start with your handkerchief.

Afterword to the New Edition

This book was born on a wet night in San Francisco in 2003, while I was escorting one of the cutest girls I know home from dinner after her show at Theater Rhinocerous. As we approached a stretch of narrowed sidewalk cluttered with construction cones, I performed a movement I'd honed over ten years—I reached across my body, took her hand that was resting in the crook of my arm, and held it out and up, then I let her get half a step ahead and more or less promenaded her through the small space. When the sidewalk opened up again, I restored her hand to my arm and made as if to continue down the sidewalk.

She stopped short, looked at me, and said, "*Where* did you learn how to do that?"

I smiled and made some sort of charming remark—I think I may have said that I'd learned it just for her—but the fact was I just didn't know. It could have been anywhere. I had been studying and immersing myself in butchness for such a long time that I had no memory of how I'd learned it. Watching and deconstructing videotapes of formal dance postures in college theater classes? Remembering how my grandfathers behaved? Working in strip clubs? Watching Leslie escort Minnie Bruce, or Ronnie escort Nancy, or my Great-Uncle Moe escort my Great-Aunt Ruth? I had no idea, but somehow it had filtered in and made its way into my muscle memory, smooth and seamless and delightful to a certain sort of girl (mostly, to the sort who shared my gender fetish, but that's a certain sort, right?).

Later, I went back to my hotel room South of Market (noticing how the leathermen walked in pairs and in packs without ever jockeying or being awkward), pulled out my laptop, and wrote "Where Butch Resides," all in one sitting, almost all in one breath. As usual, I had no idea what I was doing—I just sat down and wrote out the whole piece, somewhere between an essay and a prose poem. And then, if memory serves, it was late and there had been some adult beverages, so I promptly conked out.

While it is not possible to write a book by accident, it is possible to lurch rather far along the path without fully understanding what you're getting yourself into. I knew I was writing some essays, and sure, I'd have said I'd love to see them someday be a book, but everyone thinks ze has a book in hir. The guy who interrupted me at the library just today says he thinks *he* has a book in him too, has thought so for ten years: something like *The Da Vinci Code*, maybe, though he only saw the movie (the book is long and, well, he doesn't really like to read).

But all that tonnage of butch knowledge and identity and unexpressed feeling, once I started to look it in the eye, felt like the makings of a book if ever there was one. I discovered that the experience of butchness was yet another thing about which I had a great deal to say. And when I read excerpts at the late, lamented Boston-area open mic Gender Crash, I got a great deal of positive feedback from the crowd. And so I carried on writing it all out, using whatever craft I had, as carefully as I could, and I was very pleased when I was finished. By then I had secured a publishing contract with some fabulous friends who owned a queer small press, and we were off to the races. *Butch is a Noun* sold through its first print run (a modest thousand, but still) within just a few months.

Could we now take a moment to discuss a few things? To start with, how complicated can it be to have something you wrote in your late twenties *about your identity*, a) published, so everyone can read it, b) published, so it's out there in exactly that form in the world forever, c) published, so a lot of people with very strong feelings about your tender, complex topic can write and praise or damn you every day, and d) published, so your identity and circumstances become fixed in time?

Right. Well, it's a bit of a mess in some ways and kind of a ridiculous triumph in others—a very butch sort of a mixed bag. I haven't edited this new edition at all, except to fix typos and replace a word I used wrong. I was a bit afraid that once I started, I would never stop. Many things have changed in my worldview, and more significantly in my life, in the last six years. I couldn't imagine how to update without entirely rewriting. It felt better, and more to the point more honest, just not to break that seal. If I was wrong in the first edition, I am still wrong. That's how it's going to be.

I am no longer married to my (now ex-) wife Nicole, and I no longer live in New England. I have just recently married a fantastic guy, who I'm still pretty nuts about, and we have a brand-new baby son; also, the previously mentioned fantastic guy is a Canadian, and so I now live in Canada. There have been more books and more shows (though, for the good of all, much less poetry), a great deal more travel, new friends and the weaning away of older friends with my international move, other breakups and makeups, and all manner of changes, all against a backdrop of the things and people that have not changed. It seems this kind of upheaval is common in the period in a person's astrological timeline between twenty-eight and thirty-one. It even has a name: the Saturn Return. Oops.

And so as I return to write an afterword some years later, I consider what else I might like to say either on the topic or about the book. To prepare, I read the afterwords to some other new editions, and they seem mostly to be written by someone other than the (now deceased) author. Unwilling to be dead, or even play dead, in the service of the afterword, I thought I might just let readers in on some of the things that have gone on in the swirl around this book instead. Few things, as it turns out, are as good for generating stories as going out in the world with a book title like *Butch is a Noun*.

The thing is that when strangers—the woman next to you on the plane, your cabdriver, the bank teller, the fellow who makes your coffee, and so on—hear you're a writer, there's only one way the conversation goes, and it ends with them asking if you have any work published. In the run-up to this book's first publication, I went through a phase where I became exhausted by explaining what a book entitled *Butch is a Noun* could possibly be about (because when you say you write about gender and sexuality, there's only one way *that* conversation goes), and then fielding gender questions. So I started telling people I was writing a history of bananas.

I memorized three banana facts, of which I never got to use the third one (the strings inside a banana are called *phloem bundles* and serve to distribute the nutrients evenly across the length of a banana), and when people asked what I was working on I very eagerly announced my banana project. Whereupon they usually started to edge slowly away from me, looking as though they were being urgently summoned from a location just beyond my vantage. I counted these encounters as successes.

(Though I see that someone has recently published a history of bananas. I cannot imagine how many frequent fliers are now gesturing to that book in their local mega-bookstore, saying, "Hey, I met that guy!")

However much fun that was—and oh, it was—coming out about my work to strangers has yielded lovely things. In rural Nova Scotia I met a librarian, now a friend, who turned out to have a trans son. As unlikely as it sounds, I understand now that sometimes the world really does arrange itself for the amusement of storytellers, and that our initial conversation in the library about children's books led to an ongoing correspondence with her. When our son was born, she sent us a copy of the book *No Matter What*, the most tender, gender-free children's book I've yet seen—a gift from my favorite Maritime librarian to my then-six-day-old little boy.

There was the Amazon femme in Seattle, now also a friend, who half-jokingly proposed marriage to me at a reading, and then followed up with a remarkably astute email both thanking me for what I had written and giving an analysis of butch reactions to the book that has shaped which of these essays I read to which crowds ever since. And the redhead in Atlanta who emailed me after a reading to tell me how angry she was that I dared to call myself a butch, that she hated my book and wanted me to know that all my whining made her seriously consider returning to men (and further mentioned that if I thought I was clever with the inscription I jotted in her book, I was sorely mistaken).

Perhaps I don't have to mention that she's not become a friend.

I expected that *Butch is a Noun* would make people angry, and it has, but not in a single one of the ways I feared. I lay awake at night convinced that butches would resent my attempts to open a window into the complexity of butch experience; instead many have thanked me. I had a horror of admitting, in print, forever, that I like to get fucked, a statement I am still trying to get around in some way; even now I try out new oblique language ("not stone," "sexually reciprocal"), none of which really serves. I am not sure what I thought would happen, but I was afraid of it nonetheless. That, too, has been mostly fine, though a few snotty comments have stung more than I let on at the time.

By and large, the biggest upset seems to be represented by the email and reviews suggesting that I have categorized all lesbians as butch or femme and set The Movement™ back thirty years in doing so. I do not think I did either of those things, but everyone is entitled to their opinion. Since I tend to publish books full of my opinions, in the admittedly egotistical way every essayist must necessarily have, it seems unsporting to try to deny them their say. I would like to point out, however, since this is my afterword after all, that a book about butchness will generally be mostly about butchness and not about other genders. This is true in much the same way a book about backyard grilling is all about, well, grills. We do not assume that the author is anti-baking or harbors a long-standing animosity toward braising. If anyone cares anymore, I am certainly in favor of many other genders (and also, for the record, braising) and I still think you should do it as you prefer.

Butch is a Noun was, and remains, a book about how it went for me—not how I think it should be for you, unless what you found in the pages felt like something you wanted to move toward. In that case, I hope you have gotten enough here. There are things about which I have clearly said too much, and some about which I haven't said nearly as much as I could have (though I have tried to remedy that in later work). The people I thanked in the acknowledgments still deserve my thanks, however our relationships may have changed, and the mistakes and stupidities that crept in are still all my fault. But like Emerson (to *really* upgrade myself by association), I am now done with them, and hope to begin again with no time for my old nonsense.

The cute girl from the beginning of the book is now a beloved auntie to my son, I lost my favorite silver pocketknife to a TSA agent, and I know when I'm starting a book these days. I even begin them volitionally now. But the changes highlight the similarities, both in what I do and what I feel, between then and now. Now, as then, I feel blessed to be counted and included in the brotherhood, sisterhood, family of butches. Now, as then, I am doing my best even while I wrestle with all manner of things. Now, as then, I am trying to write my way toward understanding, and hoping the language can hitch a ride to where I've ended up.

May 10, 2010
Burlington, Ontario

S. BEAR BERGMAN is the author of two books, most recently the Lambda Literary Award-nominated *The Nearest Exit May Be Behind You* (Arsenal Pulp, 2009), and four award-winning solo performances, and is a frequent contributor to anthologies on all manner of topics from the sacred to the extremely profane. A longtime activist, Bear was one of the founders of the first-ever Gay Straight Alliance, and has watched them spread with wonder. Ze continues to work at the points of intersection between and among gender, sexuality, and culture, and spends a lot of time trying to discourage people from installing traffic signals there. Bear lives in Toronto, Ontario with hir husband and son.